THE WAYFARER

THE WAYFARER

Poetry and Etchings by
Roy Purcell

CELESTIAL ARTS
Millbrae, California

231 Adrian Road, Millbrae, California 94030

First Printing: January 1975
Made in the United States of America

Library of Congress Cataloging in Publication Data

Purcell, Roy, 1936–
The wayfarer.

1. Purcell, Roy, 1936– 2. Southwest, New, in art. 3. Self-realization in art. I. Title.
NE2012.P87A58 769'.92'4 74-25836
*ISBN **0-89087**-007-1*

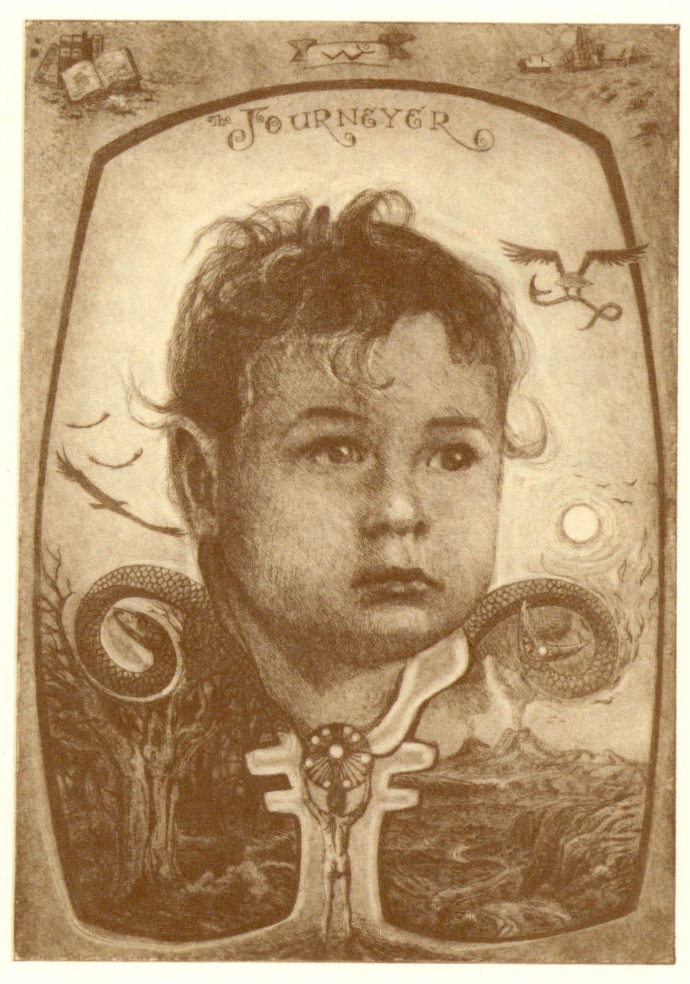

What makes a man
search the Journey that takes him
beyond the hills of home
and security
to leave both father and mother
for an unknown road

a sickness that burdens
a question that plagues
an unanswered question
the voice of Lazarus
come to take you
from the grave of norms
and a dark and inner voice follows your eyes
down the streets of childhood saying
no you'll never be a barber
you'll never be a clerk
you cannot be a farmer
no you cannot be
no you cannot
no
and so you go in disillusion
dragging a troubled mind
through years of loneliness
hoping
and all you want to do is give
when there is nothing to give
no reason to live
no hope to understand

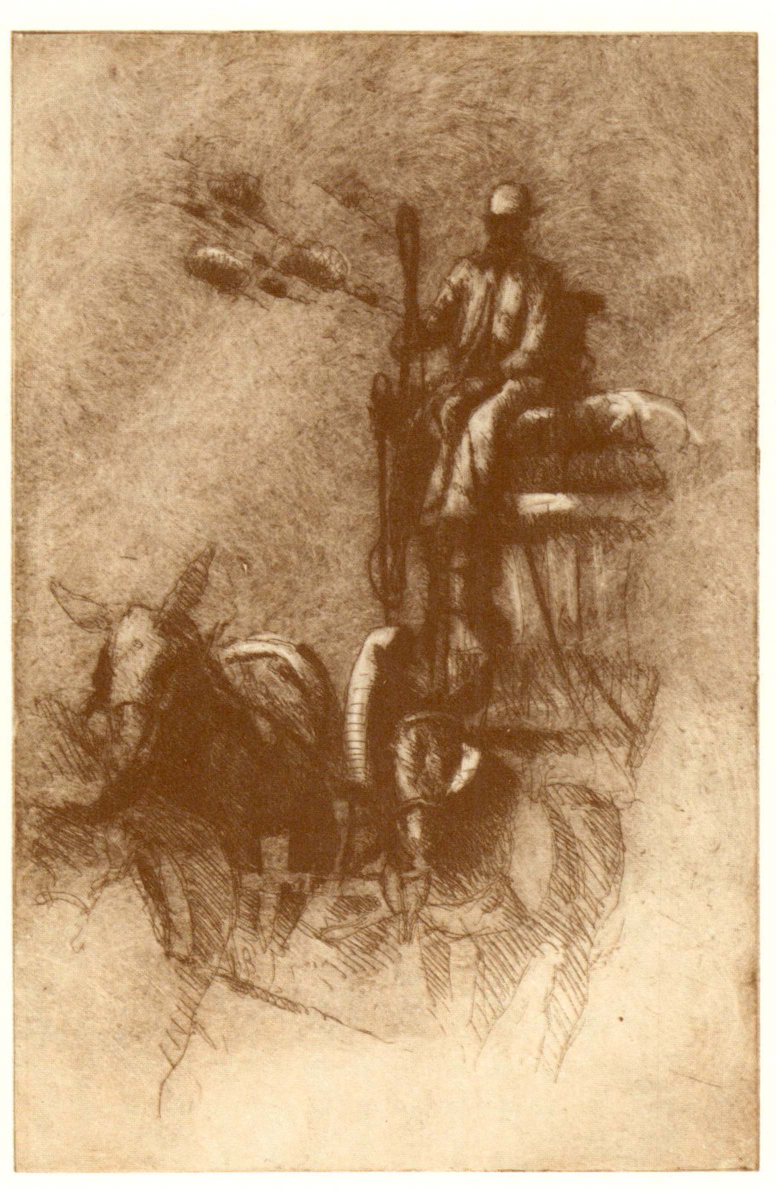

and you walk the land and pray
for a way to end your loneliness
and desolation
facing questions that have no answers
from a soul you do not hope
to understand
a prophet to yourself
without a voice
a plague to your peace
without the balm of memory
following patterns to please the ones
you cannot hope to please
and crying for love without expression
until one day a door is opened
a hand is pressed against your hand
a hope is given
a word of praise
a golden word of praise
and you begin to find the gift
that only you can give
and start your Journey

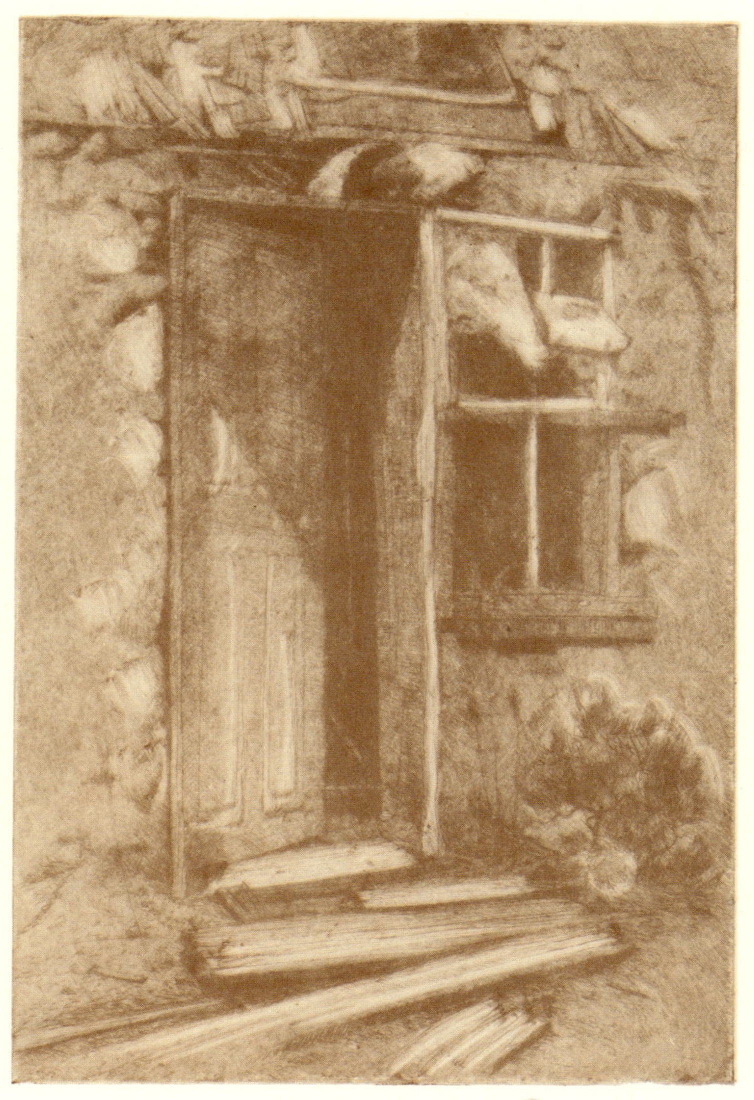

THE WAYFARER

Silence and time
have led me here
a child
and my feet know only
the Journey
the shadows of brush and stone
and twisted root
no longer frighten me
nor the breath
of wind
nor the fire
of the sun

My feet are stained
with the red red earth
through which I run
and the land
that gave me birth
is as known to me
as a faithful dog his master

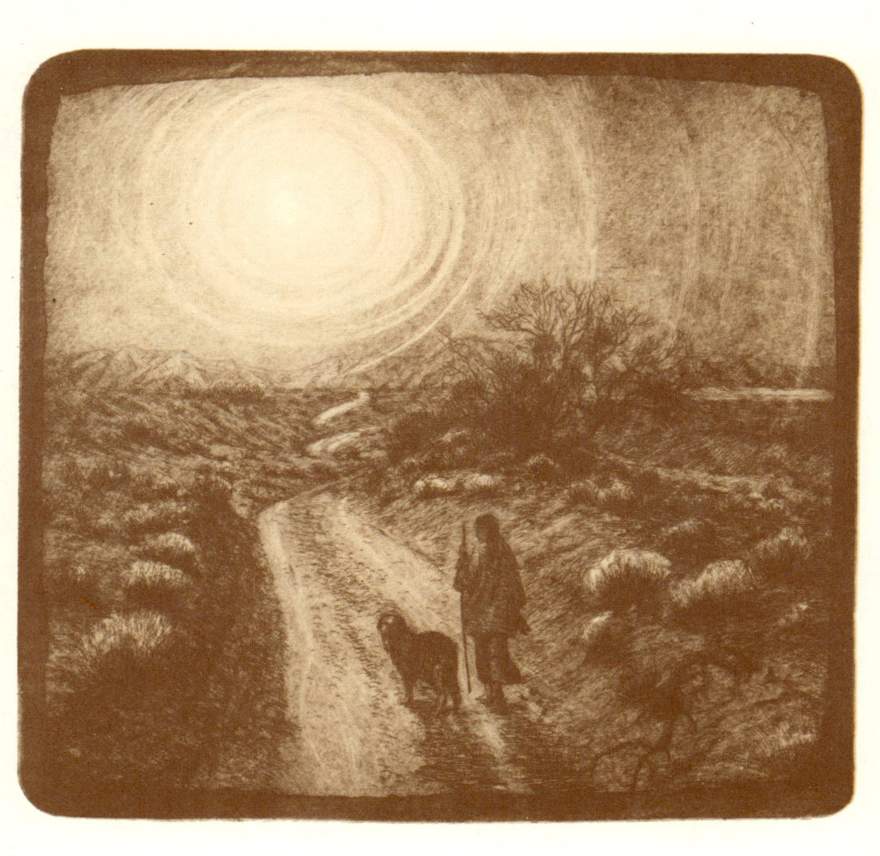

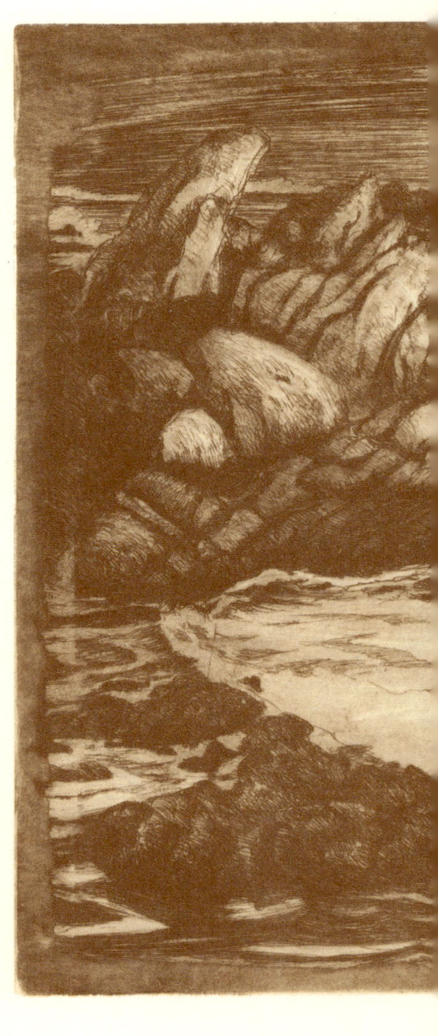

Somehow the conscious memory of birth
eludes my brain
but thoughts emerge from depths of seas within
to quell uncertainty
yet birth I knew
having come from a far country into life
through the oracle of womb that guarded
my retreat

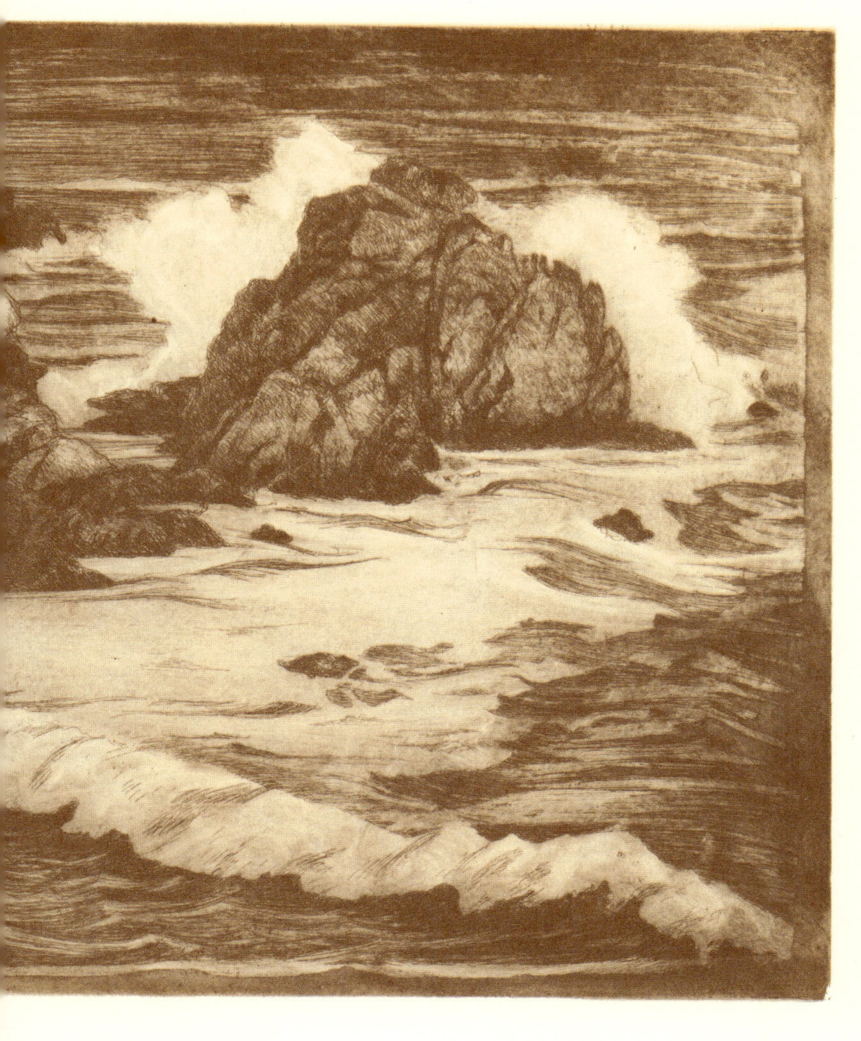

the mother's darkness did not frighten me
but warm security clustered my experience
into a Gordian knot that strangled recollection
when times's pulse pumped me
down the chambers
of my mother
to cry myself
into the light
of day
through the frightening world of flesh

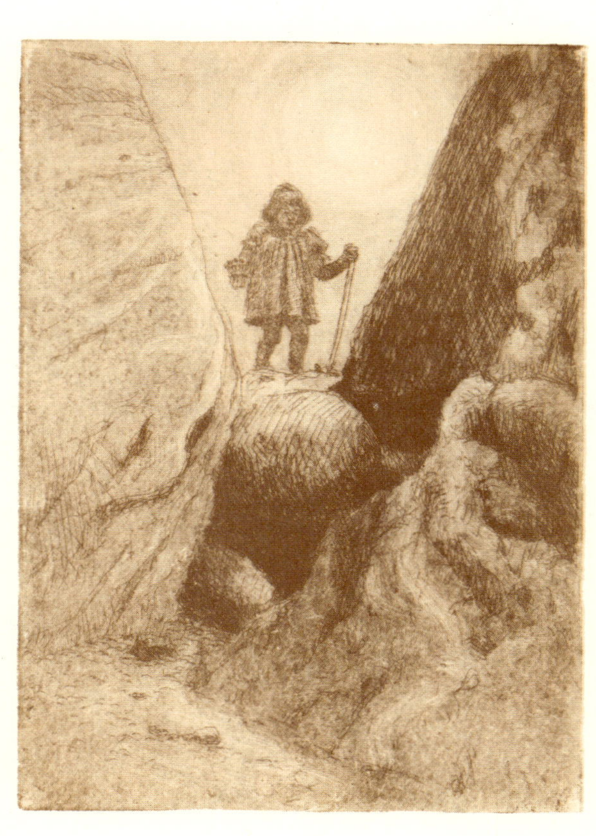

Having come as two through the gates of pain
into the form of one
I wept
chained to myself
and destined
for a search
to find the part submerged
a boy
born from the feminine womb
to wander
down the roads
of time
crawling through a cold and cruel world
on the four legs of faith
following the form of my mother
around the secure walls of womb
we called our home

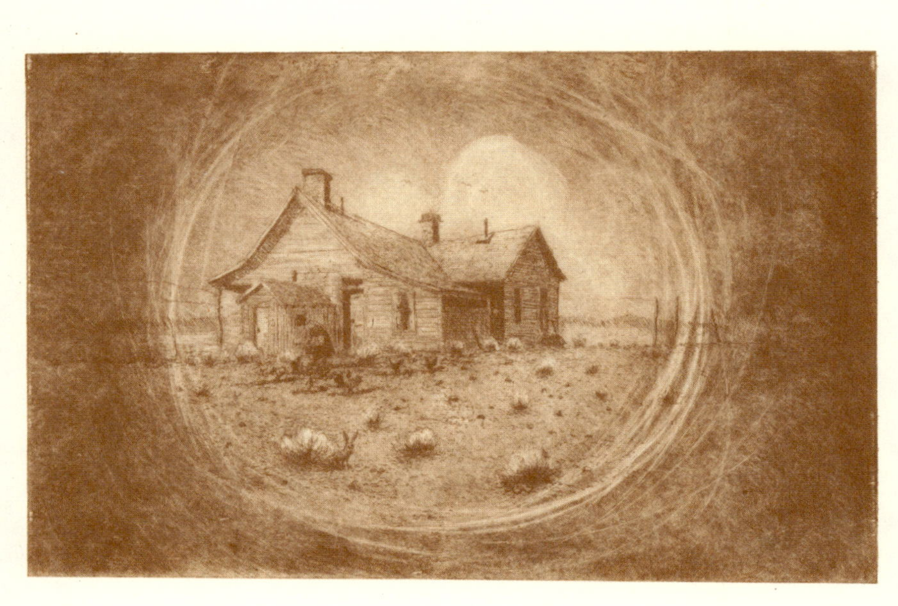

The world was huge
beyond the protective fence
that formed my prison yard
and I clung to the safety
of its security
intimidated by the sounds and images
bounding down the alien and unfamiliar streets
of childhood
a timid soul
taking its first tiny steps
into the sun

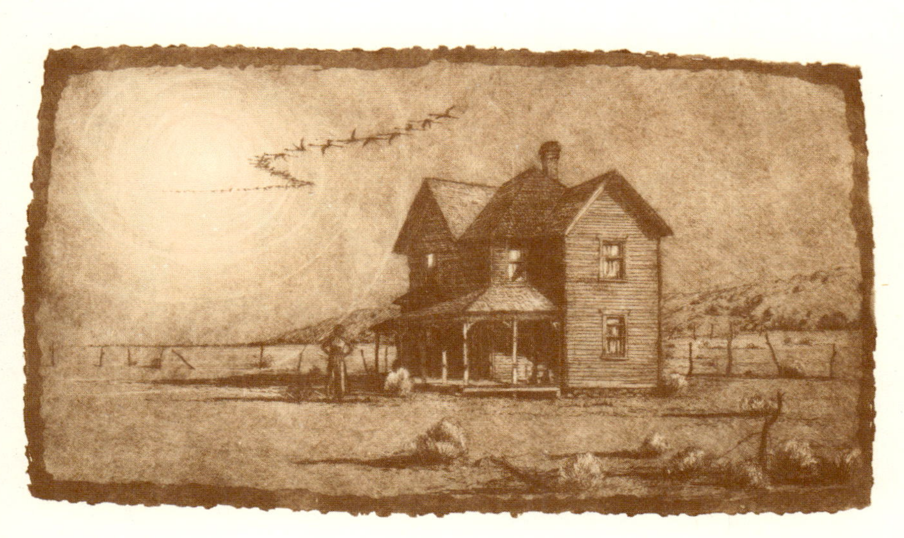

School was hell
for a soul being chipped and fashioned
into a form alien to itself
and the playgrounds of others
became the arenas of pain
in a world of cruel children
beating and screaming violence
beyond the walls of sanity
and a teacher's voice echoes
"go out and play with
the other boys"
toys for the mad
to be mocked
and broken
left lying
in the loose
red
gravel

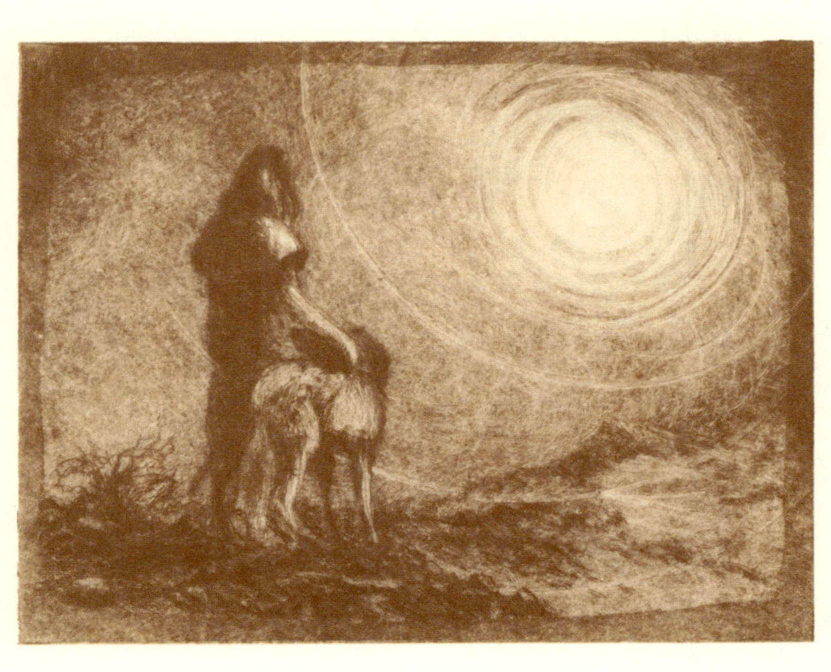

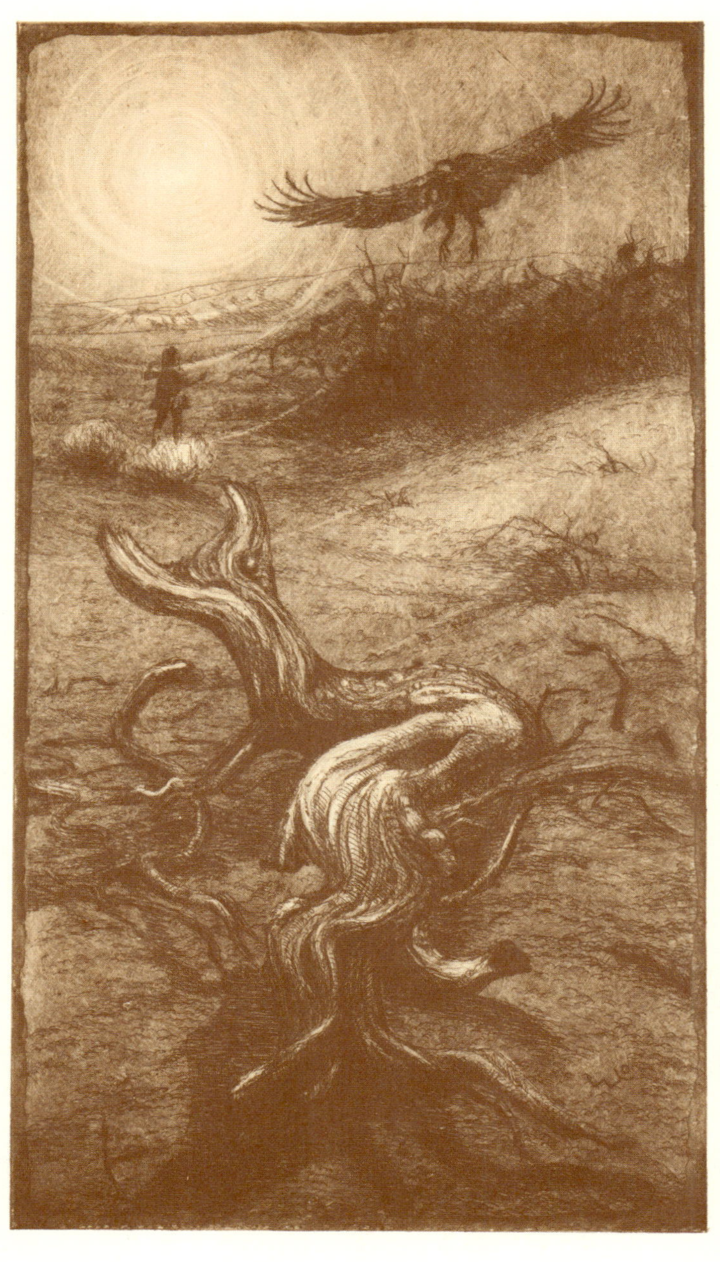

Frightened by the violence of life
in an alien world
and the overwhelming shadows
of reality
I ran
chased by the phantoms
of my imagination

Unable to cope
I came to the sanctuary of books
a cool library
quiet walls devoid of laughing children
and lost myself in the pages
of past lives
copying words and images
from the books of years
beyond my understanding

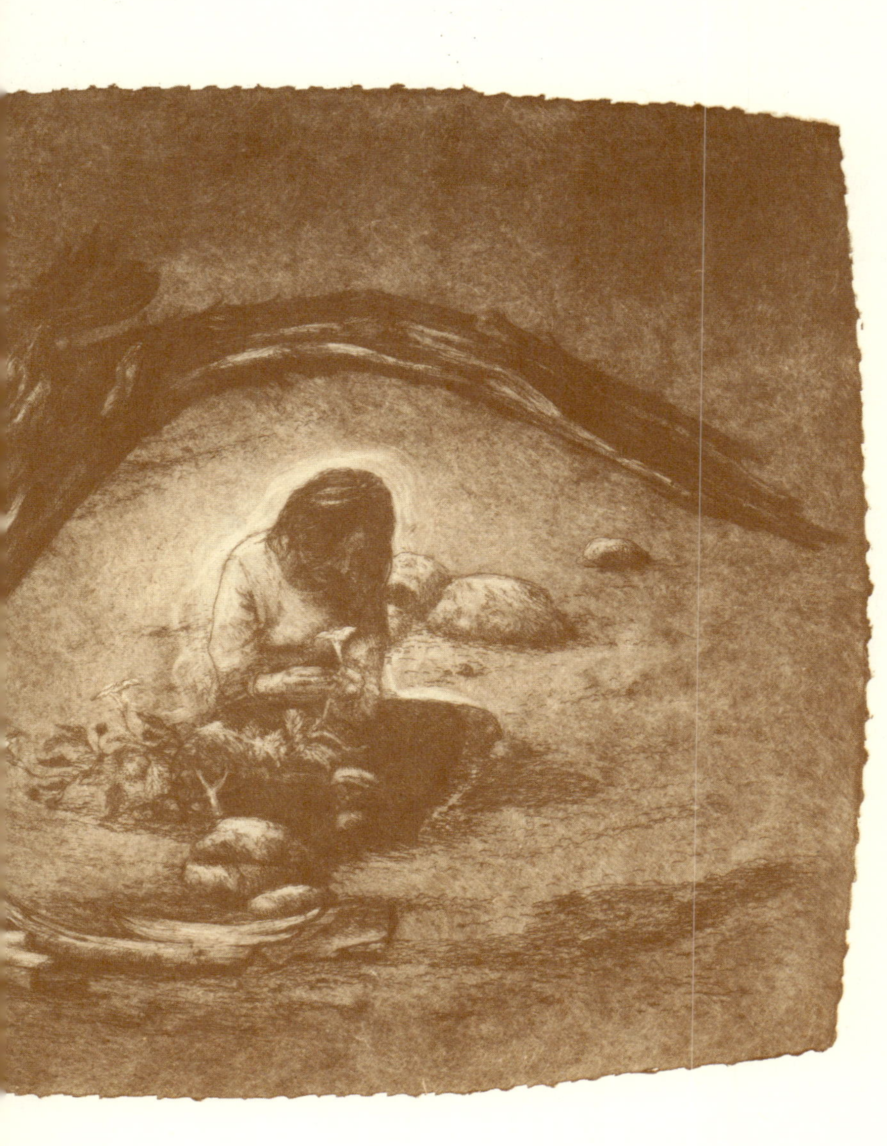

The natural world beckoned
and the pain of solitude
was eased by the voice of the wind
my sister
whispering through the leaves of summer
and my soul

A balm of soothing sadness overwhelmed me
and I wandered alone through field and forest
counting friends among the mountain sheep
and mule deer
running with bare feet
over the hills
and down the canyons
of a world apart
distant from the voices
of mocking children

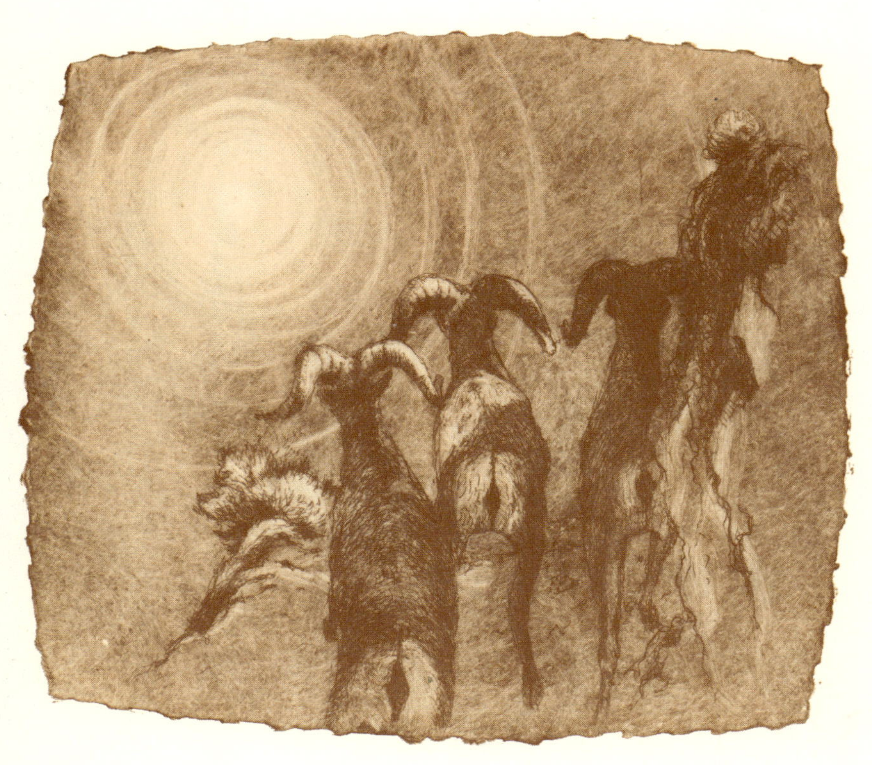

And then a voice took my hand and said
"Your grandmother is dead"
and led me down the cold dark street
a friend who hoped to share the pain
but the pain of death was no pain
a relief
a sigh of expiration
and a passing on
beyond the world of tears
beyond the sunset
where she slept
and I stood listening to weeping voices
and watched the cold face peaceful
in its hour of death
but death was not death at all
for the pain of death was mine
not hers
lying there in restful sleep
while I was feeling guilt to know my tears
were missed among the many falling
there to share their loss
at parting

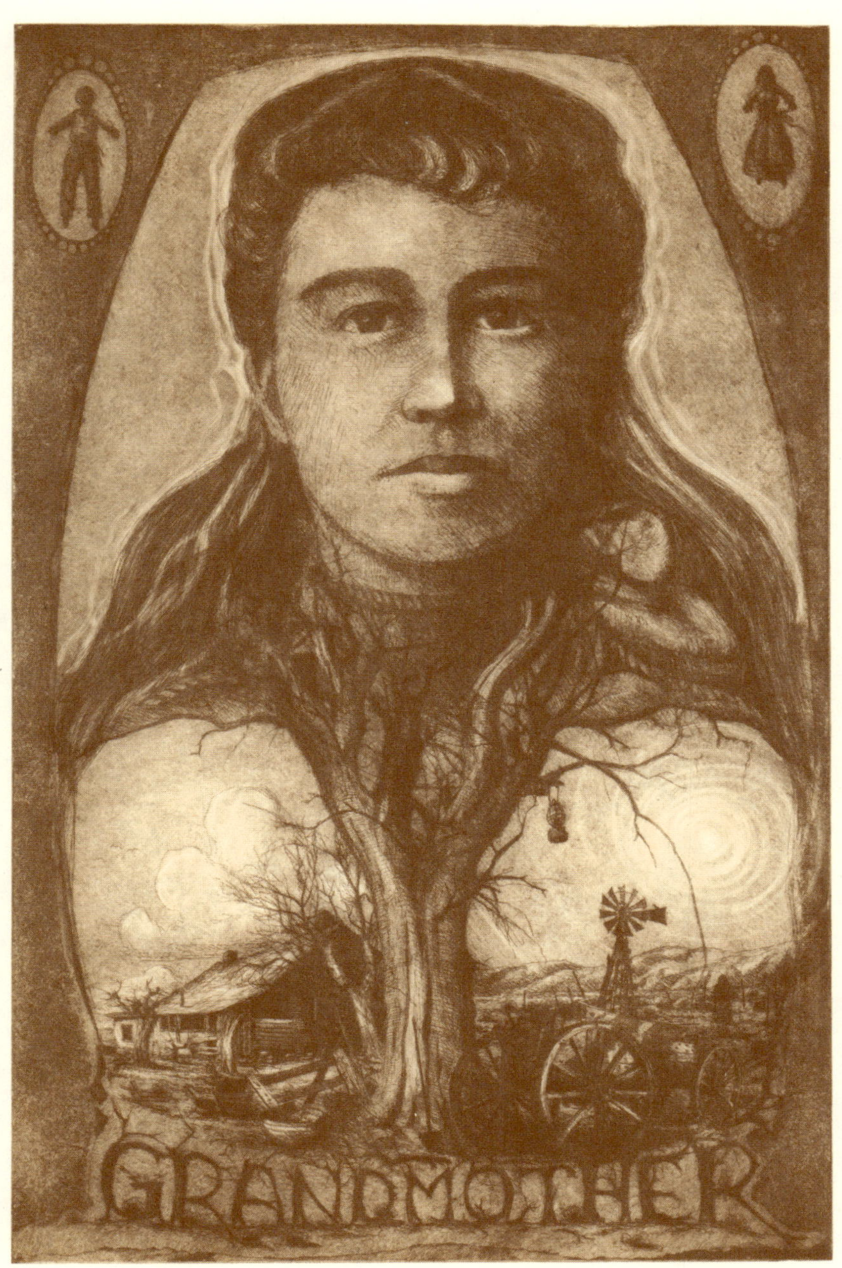
GRANDMOTHER

I found
among the voices of laughing children
a face etched deep with wisdom and serenity
calm and remote
a goddess in a little girl's form
and fell in love searching above all
a hope to hold her hand
to touch her lips to mine
to hear her voice call my name
but she was eight as I was eight
and full of fears at forming words of praise
so down the years I marvelled
full of love entombed without expression
crying to express the inexpressible
beneath the cataract of fears
cascading down my soul
until one day
after years had passed in painful admiration
gaining courage out of sheer necessity and silence
I wrote upon a torn piece of precious paper
the beautiful and magic words
I LOVE YOU
held it close for days awaiting circumstances
that would take my love to her
and seal the unformed bond that formed
the bondage of my frantic hopes

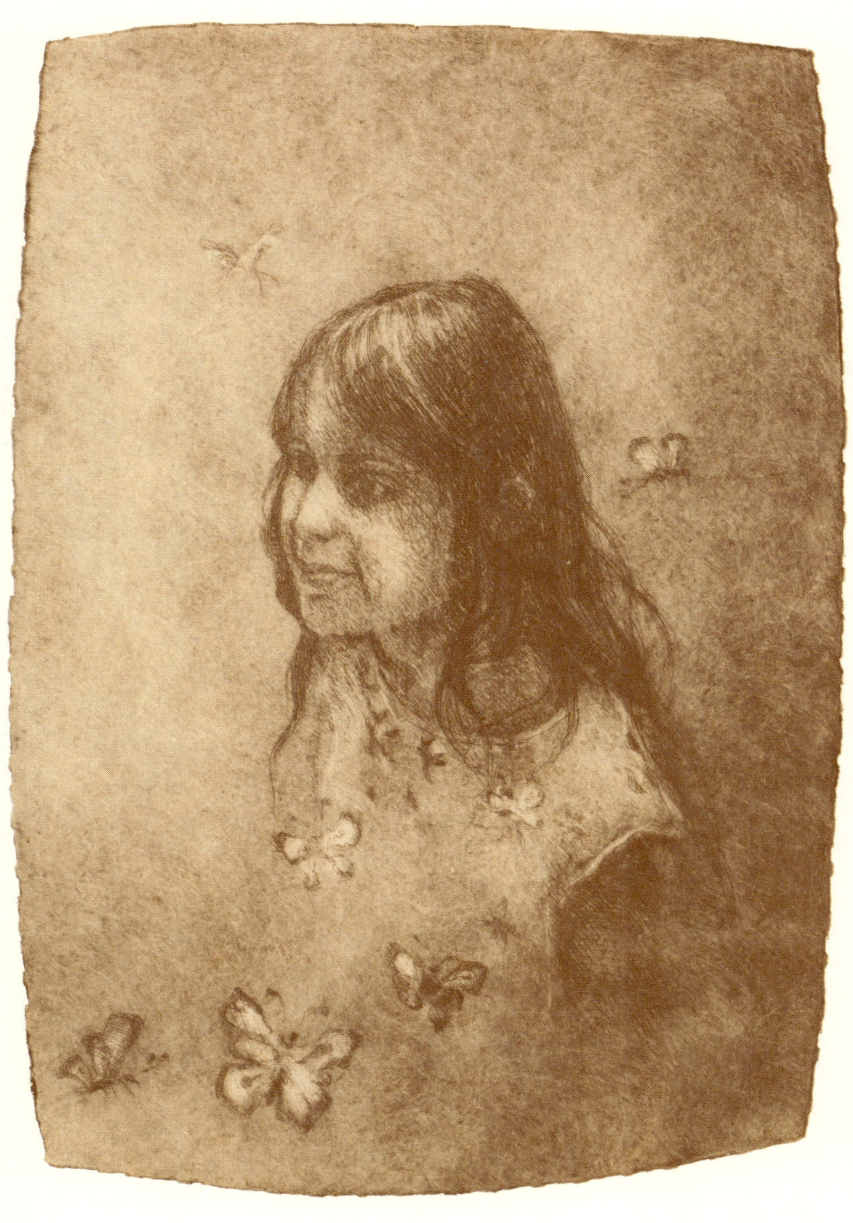

And then one day
she stepped in silence from a silent door
to where I stood in wonder in the hall
the confrontation

I slipped the precious note
into her unexpecting hand
and turning ran the echoing empty hall
around a distant wall and waited
turning in fear to see her
hold the opened note before cold eyes
crumple it without expression
and drop my heart upon the concrete floor

No more would I love
never let my heart find hope
within another heart
and inexpressible loneliness
sent me drifting
down the years of time
and growing
and I wept

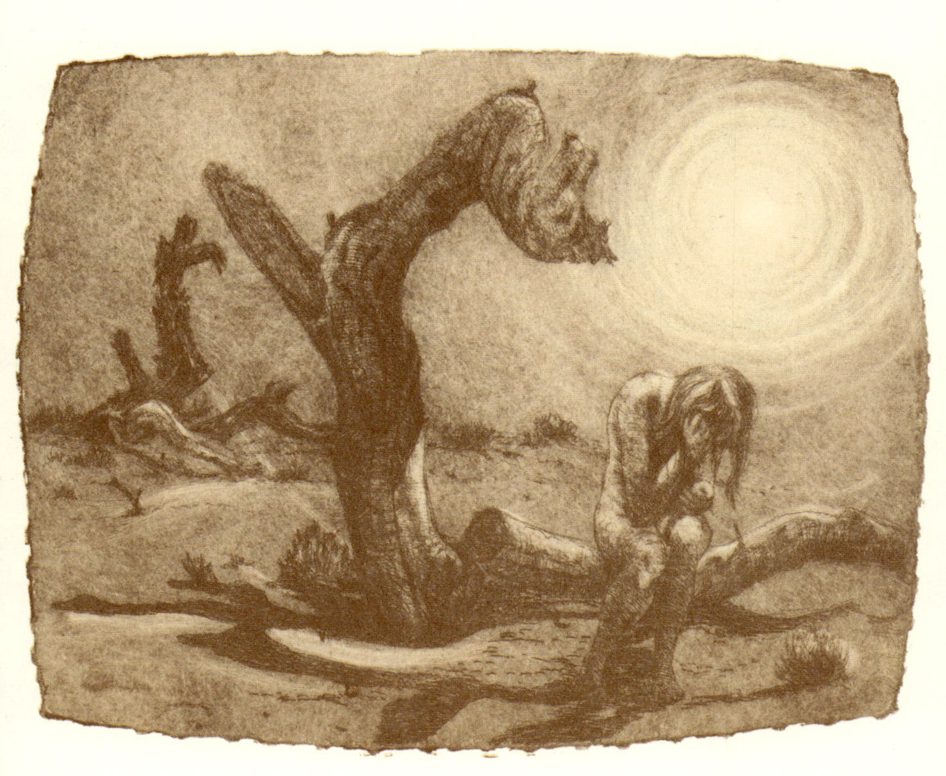

Puberty had probed its way
into the
corridors of my being
sending vipers in search of vacant holes
among the rocks
of my imagination
building tension with the nets
of new and unfulfilled desires
and I ran
searching release
from a body gone wild

Time became a dual torment torn with strife
and the early fields of my freedom from pain
became the battleground
of a new form of fear

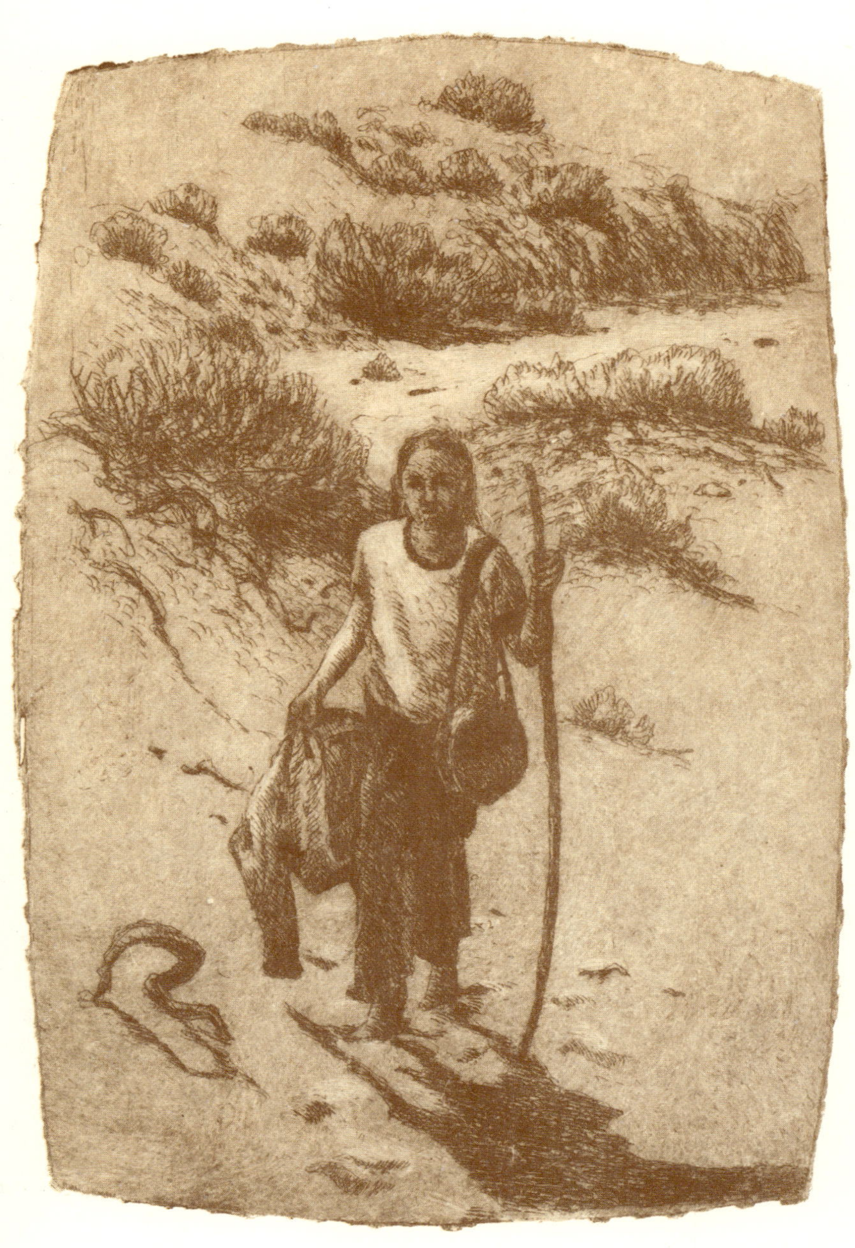

The holy hills where I had run
to be alone
now held the terrors
of an agonizing loneliness
desire for fulfillment and the fear of confrontation
had fashioned a prison
from the fires of my emotions
and melted the steel of my being
waiting to be structured upon the anvil of life
the holy God of heaven had cursed me
sent howling on a pilgrimage of anguish
and internal strife

Searching a hope for being what I could
I found myself before a colony of ants
along the lonely streets of childhood
and lying there before the mound's activity
observed the scurrying in and out
as each ant traced its task upon the sand
echoing questions in a soul that had
no answers
and answering no questions
for my troubled mind

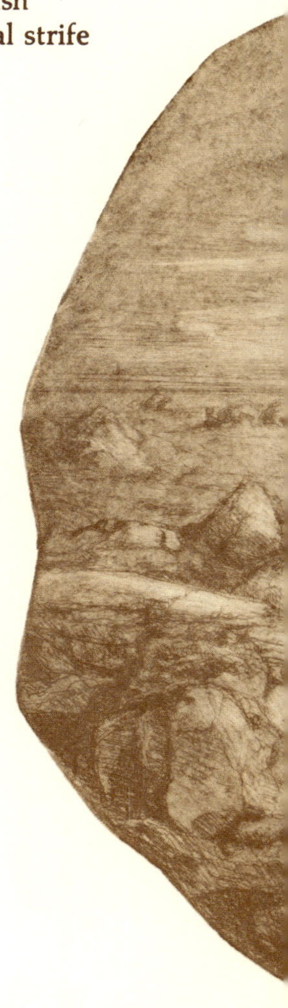

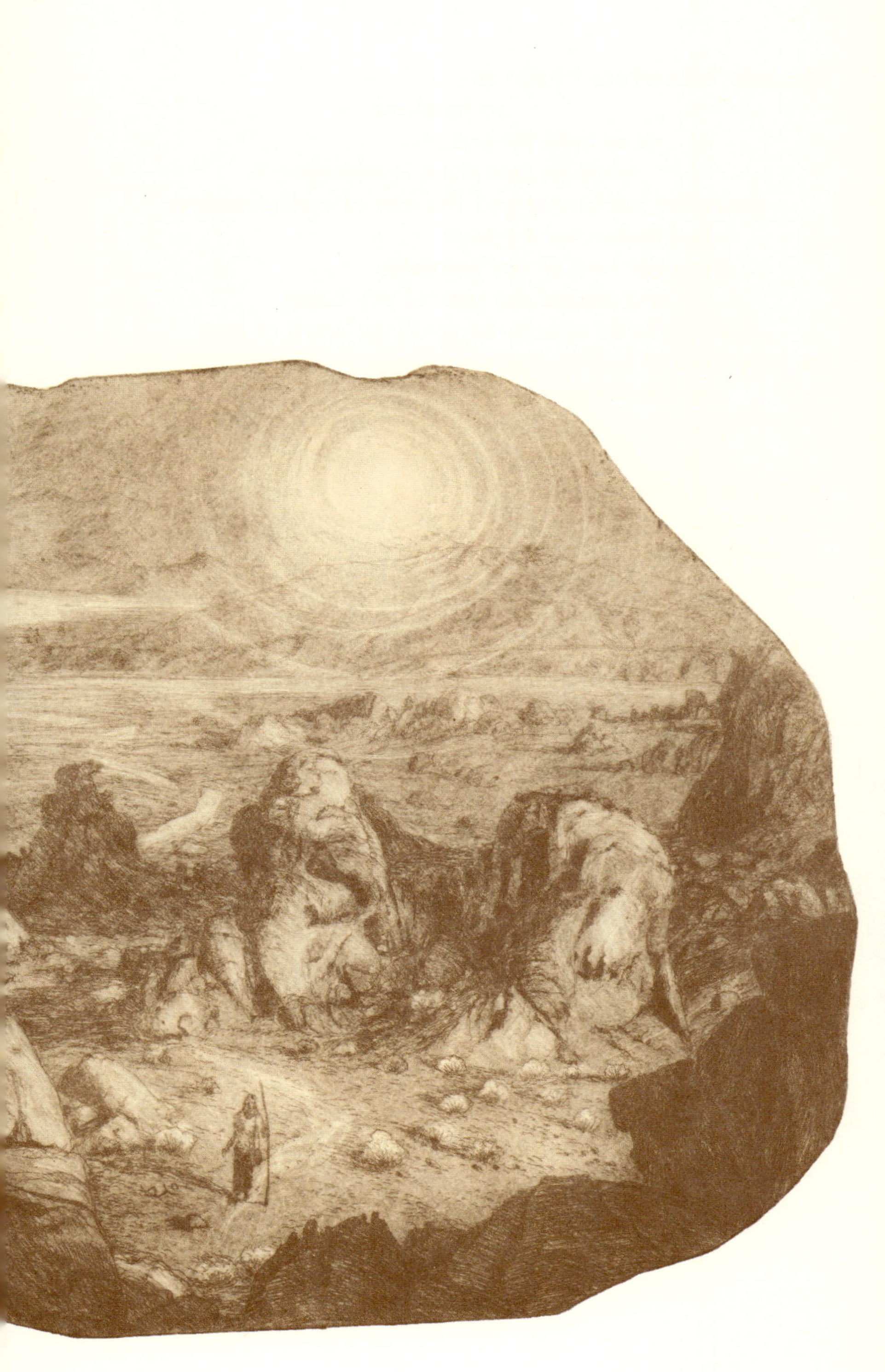

I could not be a worker carrying grass
from my fields of longing
through the empty streets to feed the cattle lowing
in the sheds of home
nor structure the tunnels of passage
down the labyrinth of life
in the outer world of flesh
that cradled me
could never guard the gates of sand
against the hand of enemies
I could not hope to know
protecting a mad world
from a further madness
could only drone my hours to the queen of hearts
to die upon the drop of eggs
and crucify my coming
down the chambers of royalty entombed
or bear a burden of leaves to form
her couch

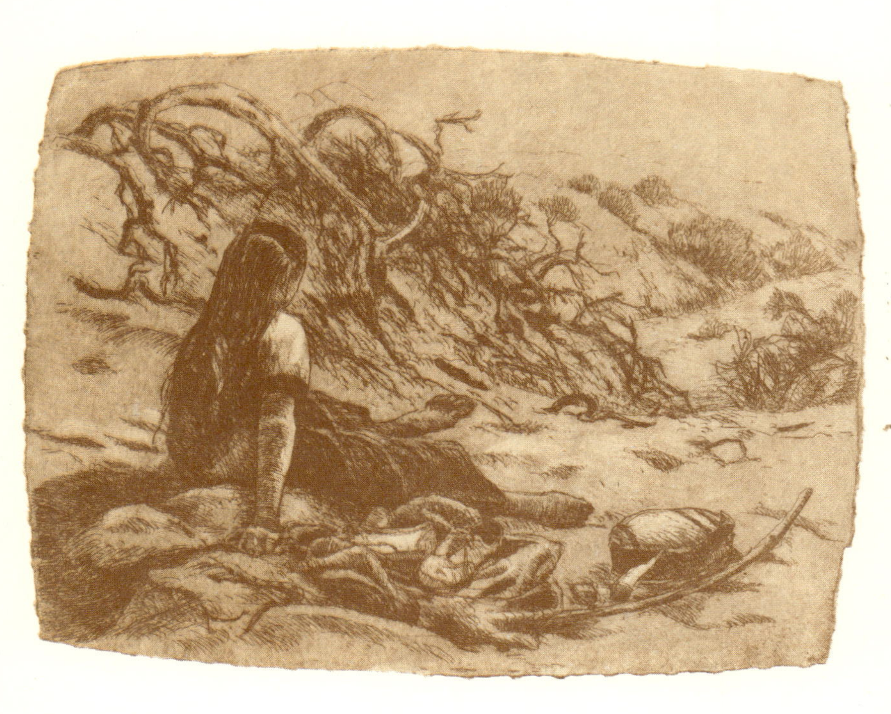

Cold hands controlled the coming arts
expression unlimited lying there in depths
I feared to tread
unknown gifts beyond the bed of dreams
untouched
as flesh and mind were taught
to choose a task
and down the roads of shame
I came with pen in hand
a gift unwanted
a desire for directions unknown
knowledge unneeded
talent unheeded
trying only to please
and crying
would someone somewhere
out there please reach in
and touch?

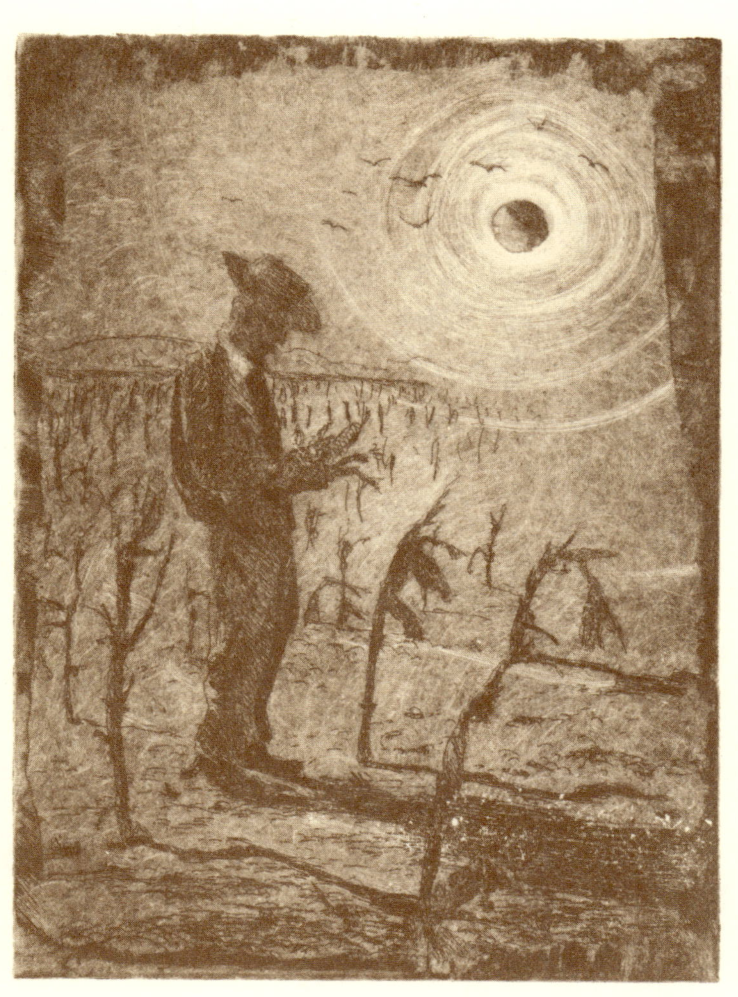

And finally someone did
a door was opened
a smile spoke in silence
and I entered
a quiet haven of solitude within the walls
that formed the youthful halls of learning
a womb of forms reflected from a simple pen
and there my gift was graced with praise
a hope was given

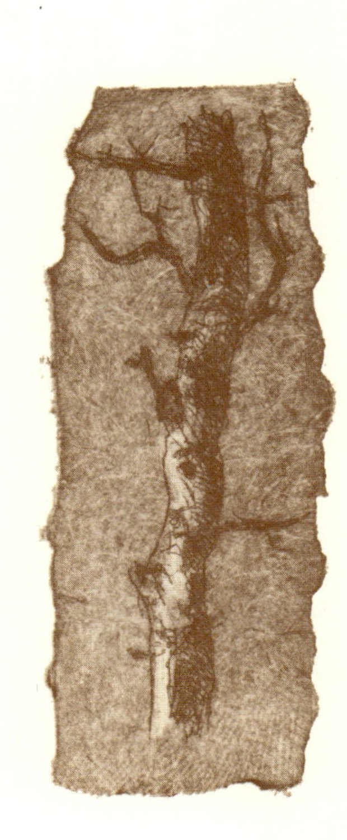

I lost myself in images of forms
exchanging reality for illusions
found amid the hills of home
devoid of the pain of confrontations
following paths of longing
down the fertile fields
of my coming
and raised my battered soul
above the heads that mocked
and breathed my first cool breath
of crystal air

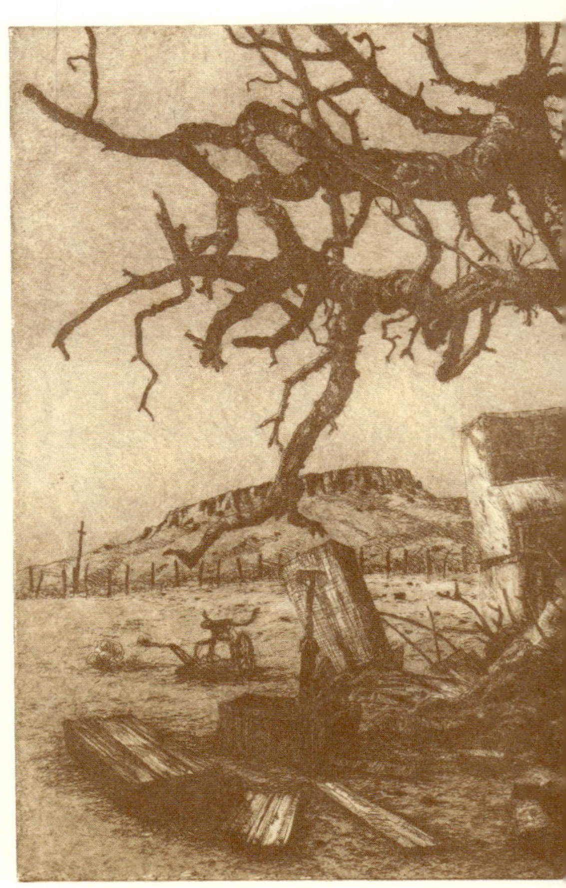

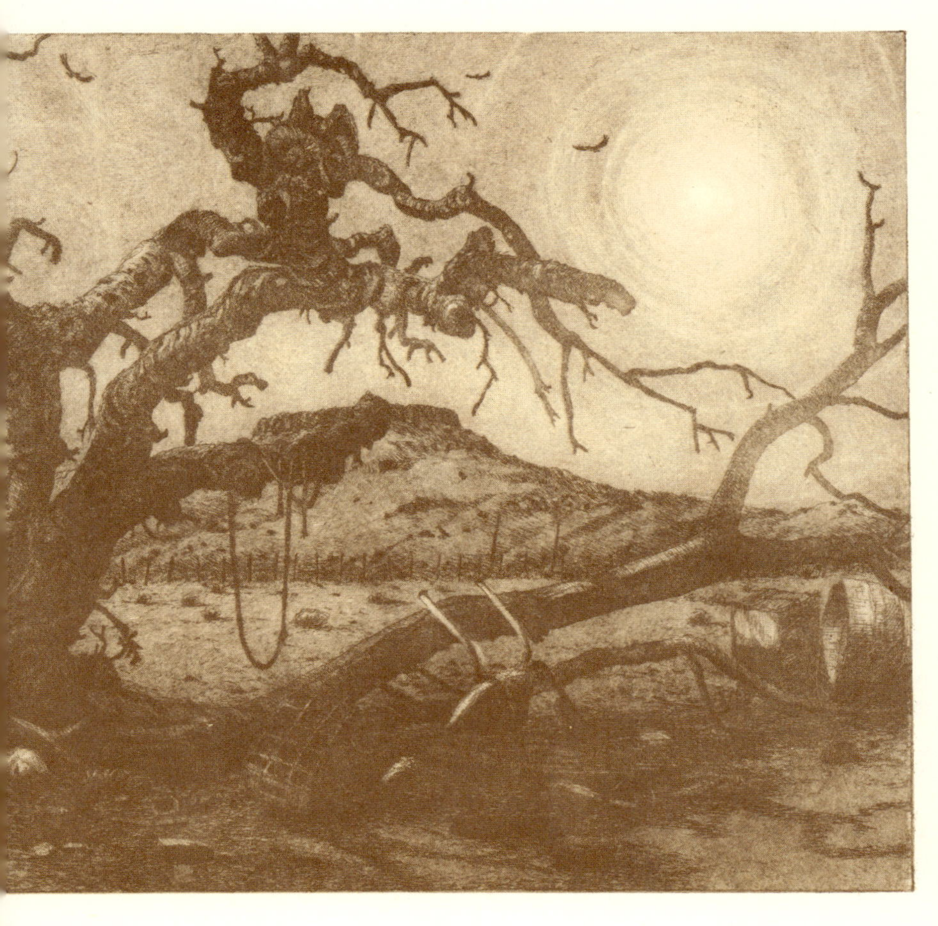

And then it was over as I walked
beyond the eagles aerie
and the strains of auld lange syne
and duty carried me on iron wheels
into the signs of war
that left me drifting
on the distant beach
of time
playing games of violence
to a song of hate
trained to curse and fight to kill
another me on another hill
and my body and soul
learned to separate
a lonely spirit alienated from the flesh
in fear
by acts of undeserving cruelty

I drifted
watching my self
trudge the mud through nightmares marvelling
at the bestiality of man
the base contemptibility of egos soaring

on the cloth stripes of authority
and sensuality satisfying itself
in the gutters of filth
running down the streets of an alien land
and wished *I* could. . .

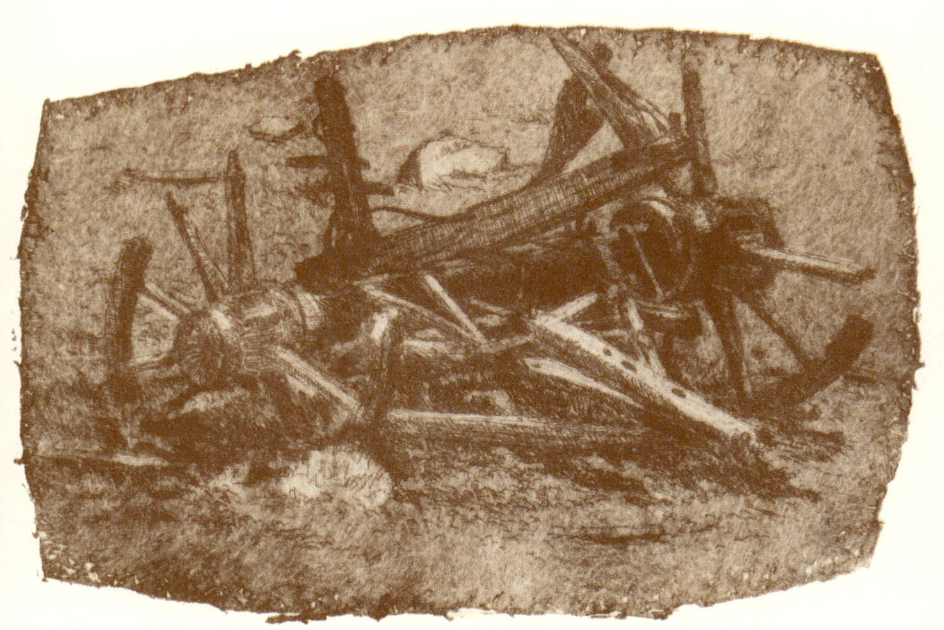

But rain fell in never ending torrents
in my sealed mind
and I found myself divorced from reality
drifting without direction
through the structure of a dead world
in search of sanity

I came to feel the eyes of love
across a crowded room
a touch of gentle fingers searching silence
a reprieve from horrors remembered
among the dreams of moon upon the sands
and the sun illuminated trails down my coming
to ease the pain
awakening seeds of dormancy
that sent my restless soul
searching images of life in the fertile fields
of my longing

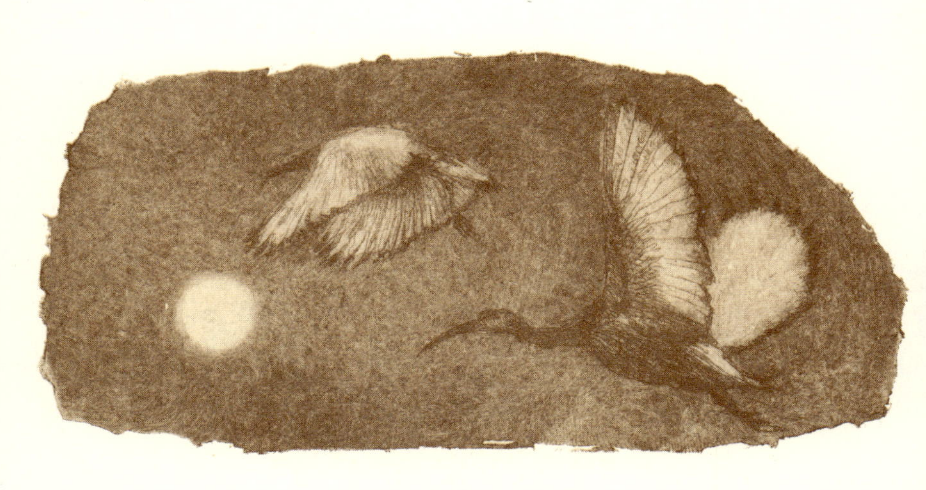

Paths of training led me down a search
through souls converted to a path
I could not tread
hoping to find direction
among the Christian dead
and days pushed on beyond the walls of nights
that knew my frantic search for the light
of faith
devouring books and angels in a hunger for heaven
heated by the fire
that drove the prophets
into the ancient hills
to hear the thunder of God's voice
rolling down the ages from Mount Sinai
beckoning me
beyond the empty halls of love
and overshadowing the dove
that hovered
in the holy air of faith
before the gates of paradise

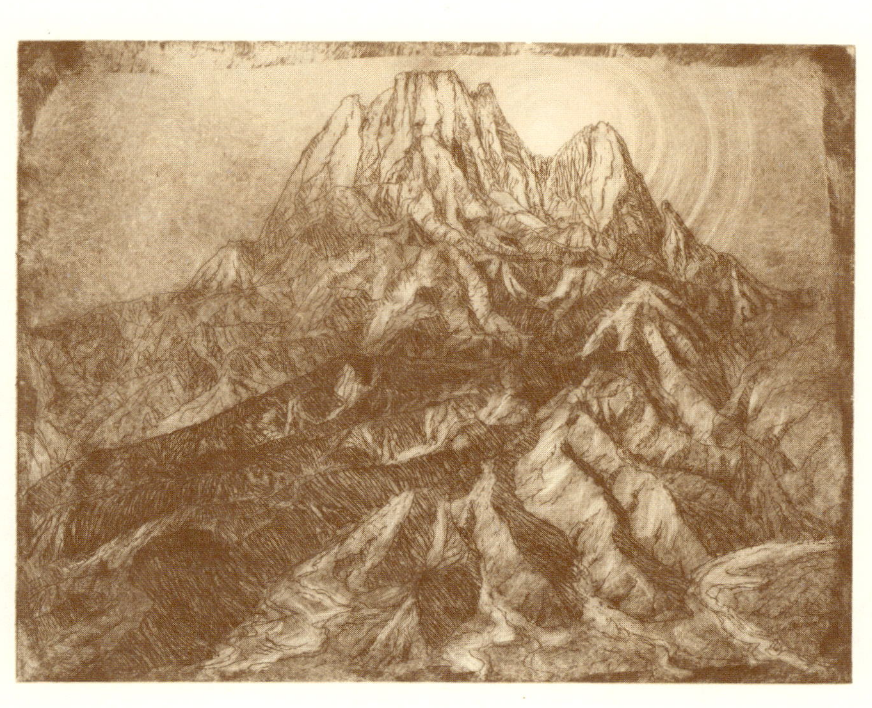

Down I plunged
intrigued by sacrifice
and caught
in the cruelty of fear
I fell before the fatal light of learning

Christ was overshadowed
by the billowing voice of Yahweh
echoing in the empty chambers of my soul
and I left the green pastures
of Christian praise
to search my own voice
and a mate
among the broken rocks
gathered at the base of my being

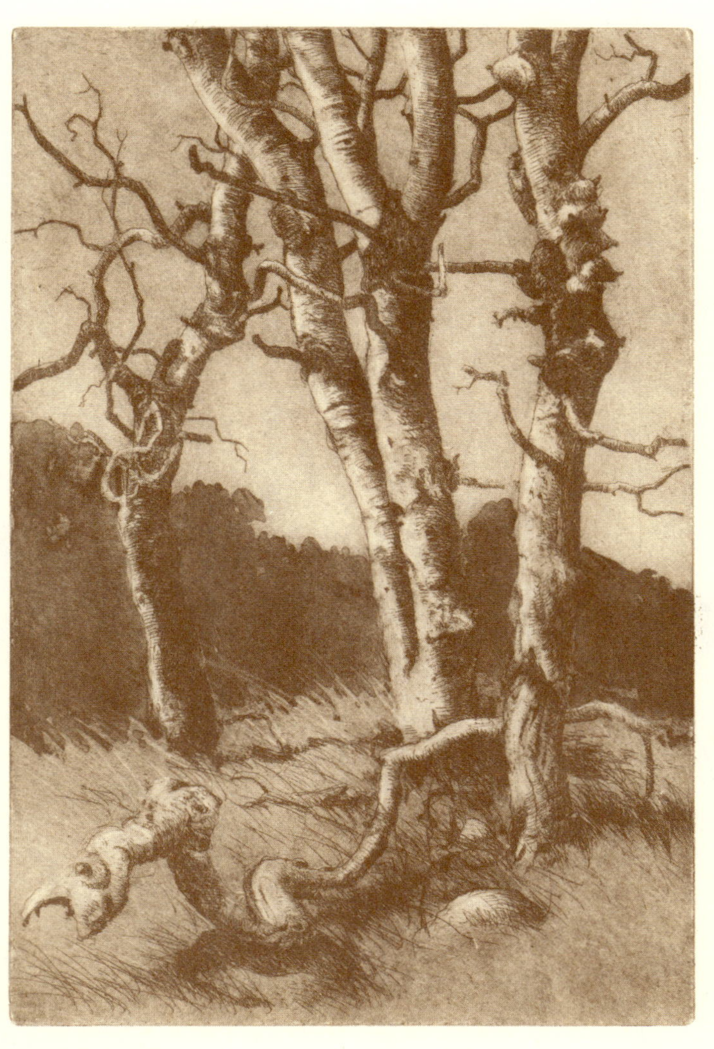

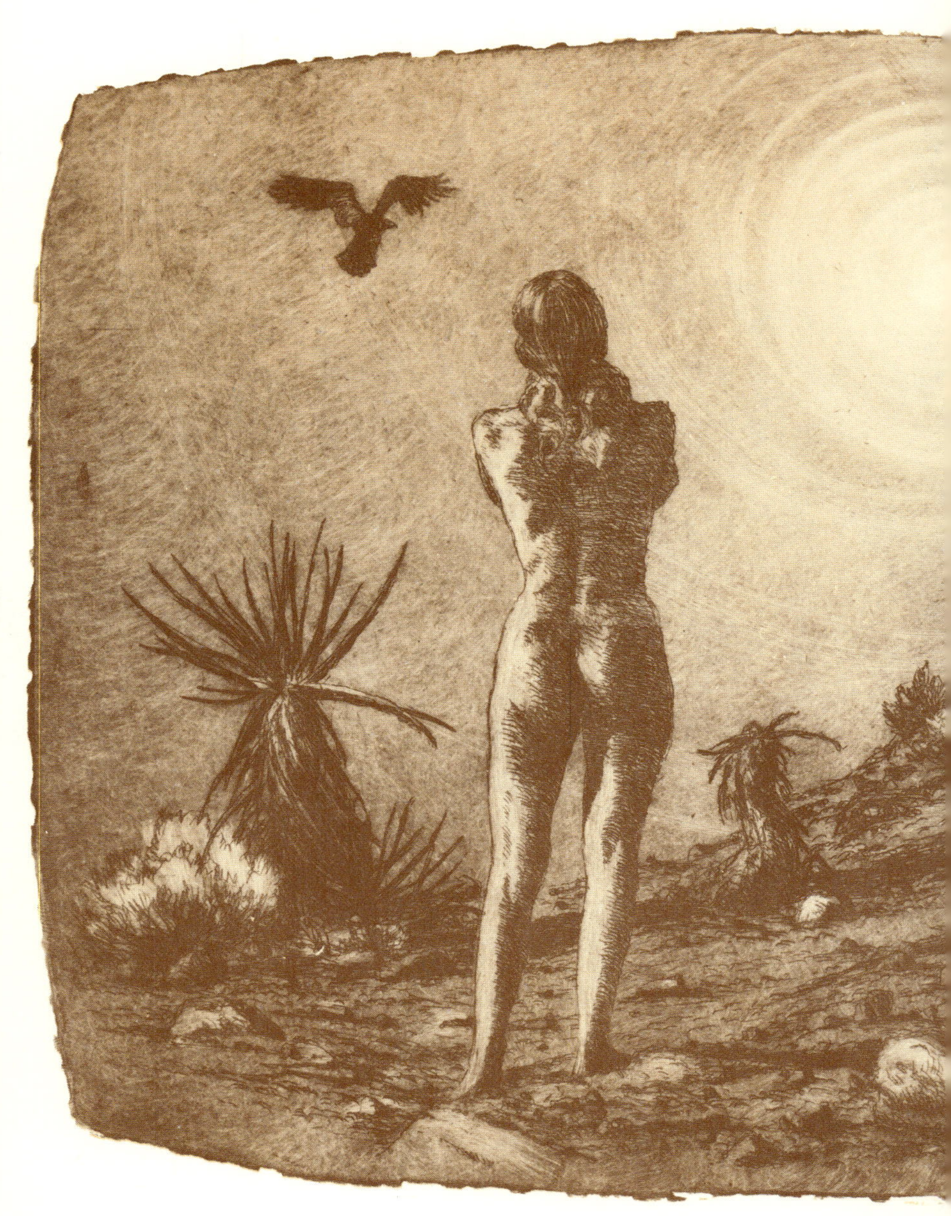

Marriage was holy but remote
distant as dreams
fulfilling
and elusive as the streams of ice
that flow from glaciers down
to the warm warm sea

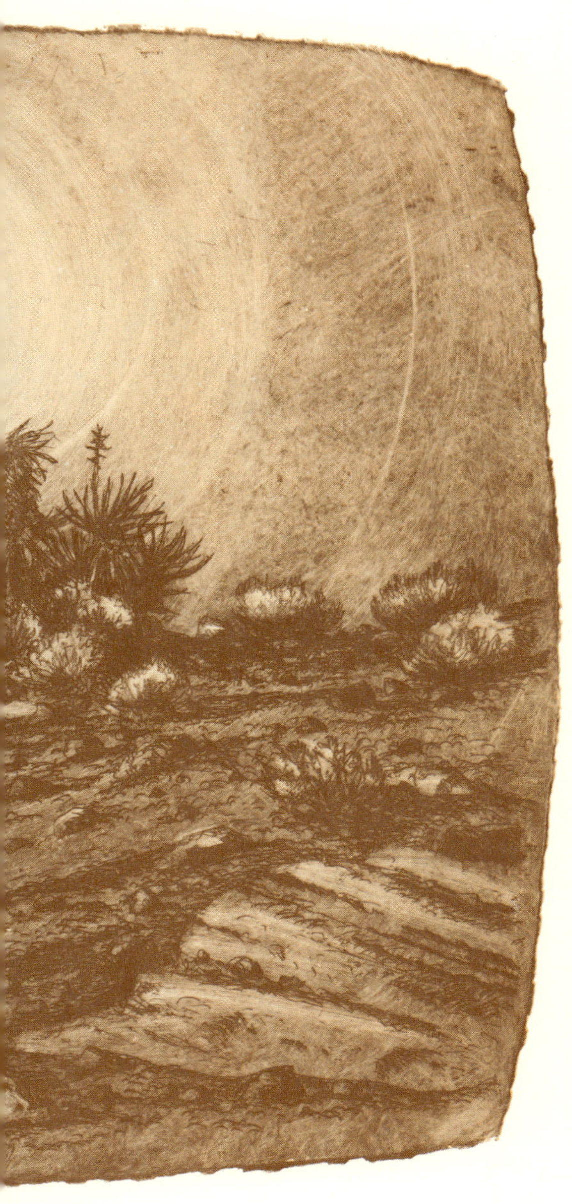

A settling of restless feet
for dim directions
and a desire for growth
based on the bed of love's security
for a head filled with vague
and unknown dreams
that led me past the portals
of reality
trailing the Ariadne thread
into the darkness
of the coming world

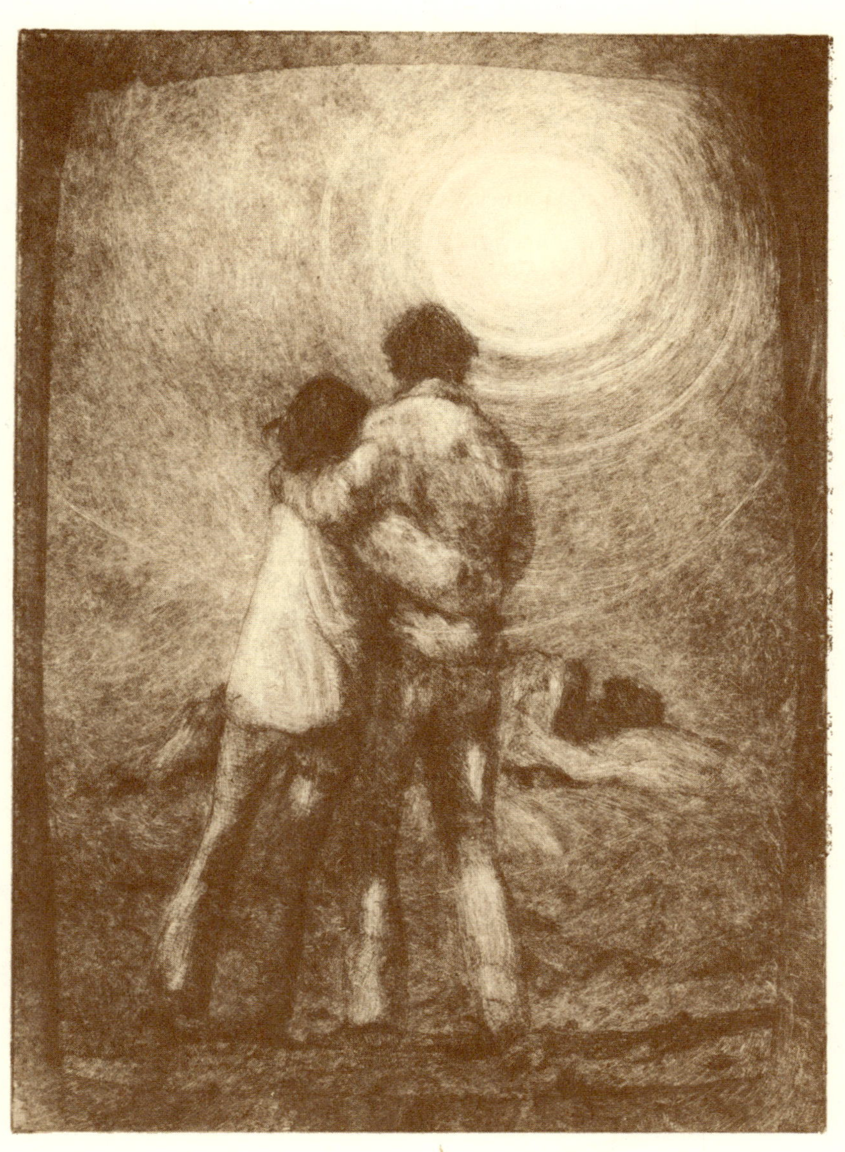

Again to the land of books I came
amid the ivory towers of learning
down the halls of fame and voices
distant and decisive
on the written page
a game of facts and faces
from an open book
a look at worlds beyond the worlds
that knew my coming
while an inner voice called my name
carved it upon the cliffs of time
elusive as the light that guards the day
while voices of security were heard to say
"do not hear them
do not listen longer
do not go
into the darkness
of the womb
the tomb of trails that lead
beyond the firm foundations
of your faith"
but the voices of friends and family faded
jaded by the pressures
of unfulfilled desire
bubbling up
from that dark land of dreams

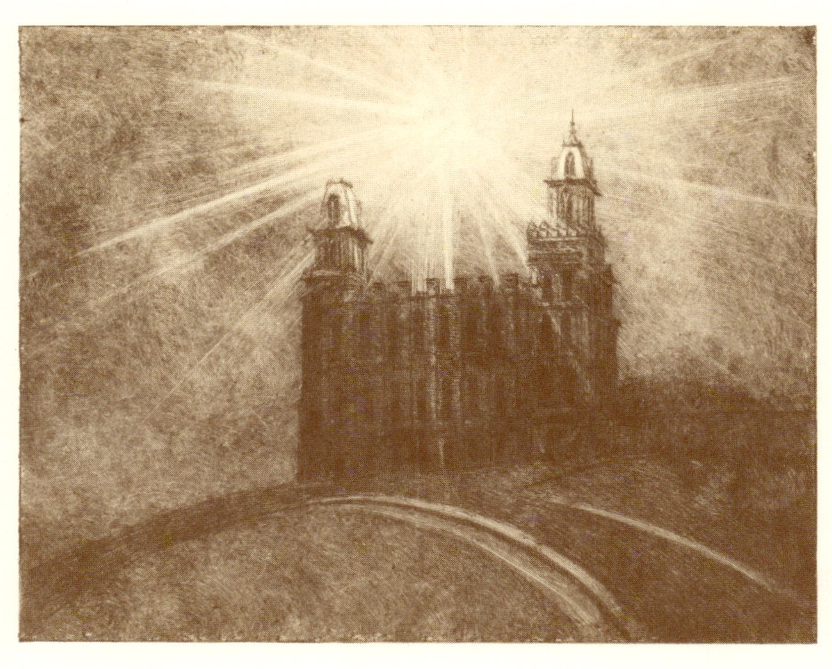

With brush in hand
I wandered through the land of forms
with fractured eyes
to see what I was taught to see
but forms of dreams emerged
within the forms
and broken buildings rusted
by the sun
became the rusted buildings of my soul
revealed by sun and shadow
and my hand stroked images
with camels hair and paint
upon the paper pages of my days
reflections of illusions
revealing the space
between illusions
in the land of dreams

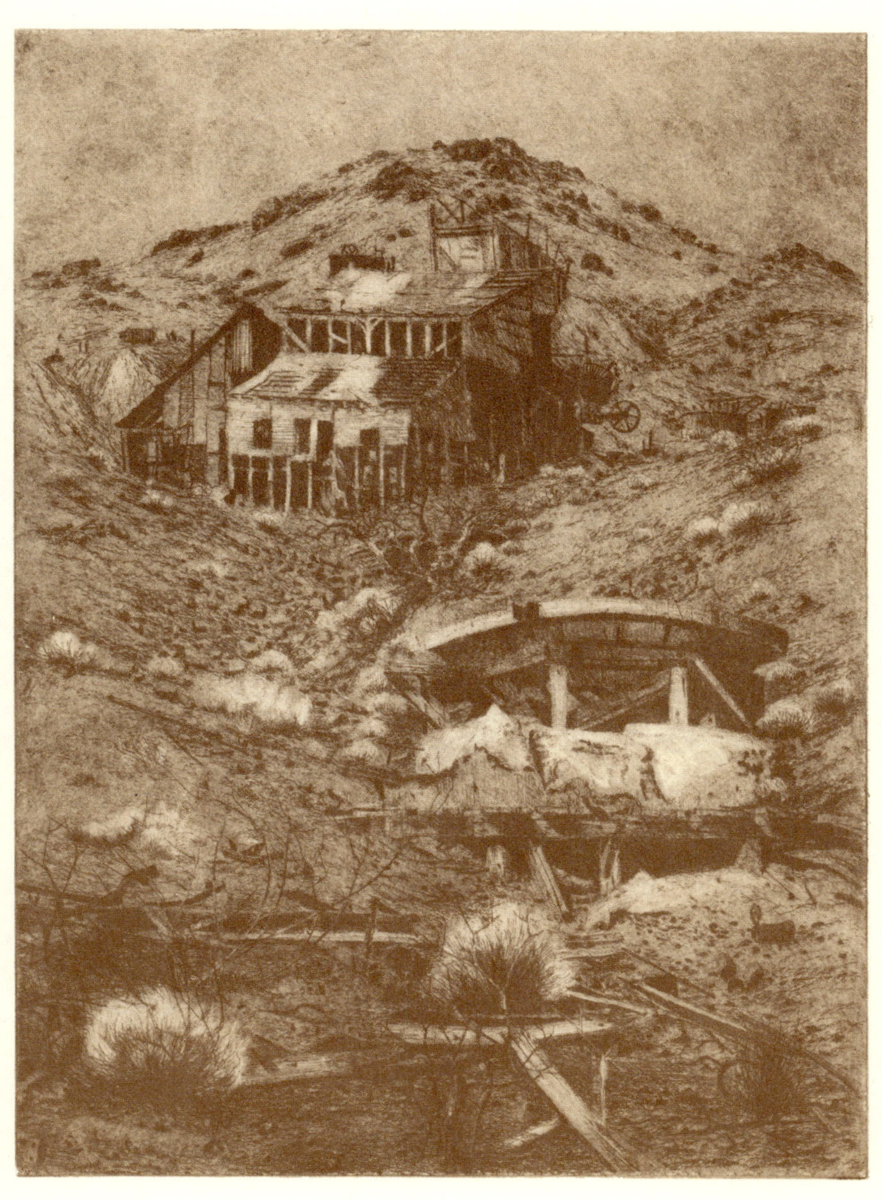

And voices
from the cloistered halls of repetition
halls of learning
bounced from ear to ear
"do not hear them
do not go
into that land of dreams
do not paint the streams within
the streams illusion
lying beyond the face of forms"
and as I ran descending down
the endless days that cried relief
from tension's bonds
the voices faded
gifts held out in hands of promise
faded
"what are you going to be
what are you going
what are you
what. . ."

amid the pennies offered as a slut
for portraits of our fading flesh
I would not
could not be professional
a portrait man
designer
artist in residence to train
the teachers draining students down
the visions of dissected dead

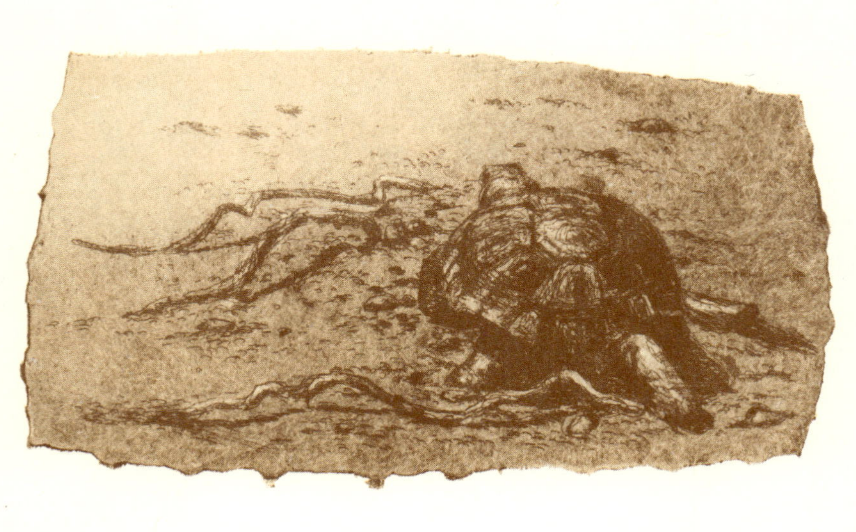

could not sustain the dreams of yesterday
and fled the voices
that clutched at dead security
the voices that mocked
and followed
the voices that lured me
into the lonely deserts
of my slow becoming
the crucible
of what I could
and somehow
someday
would

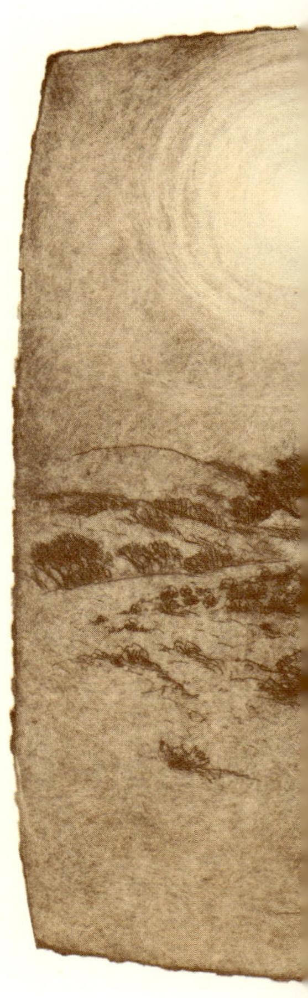

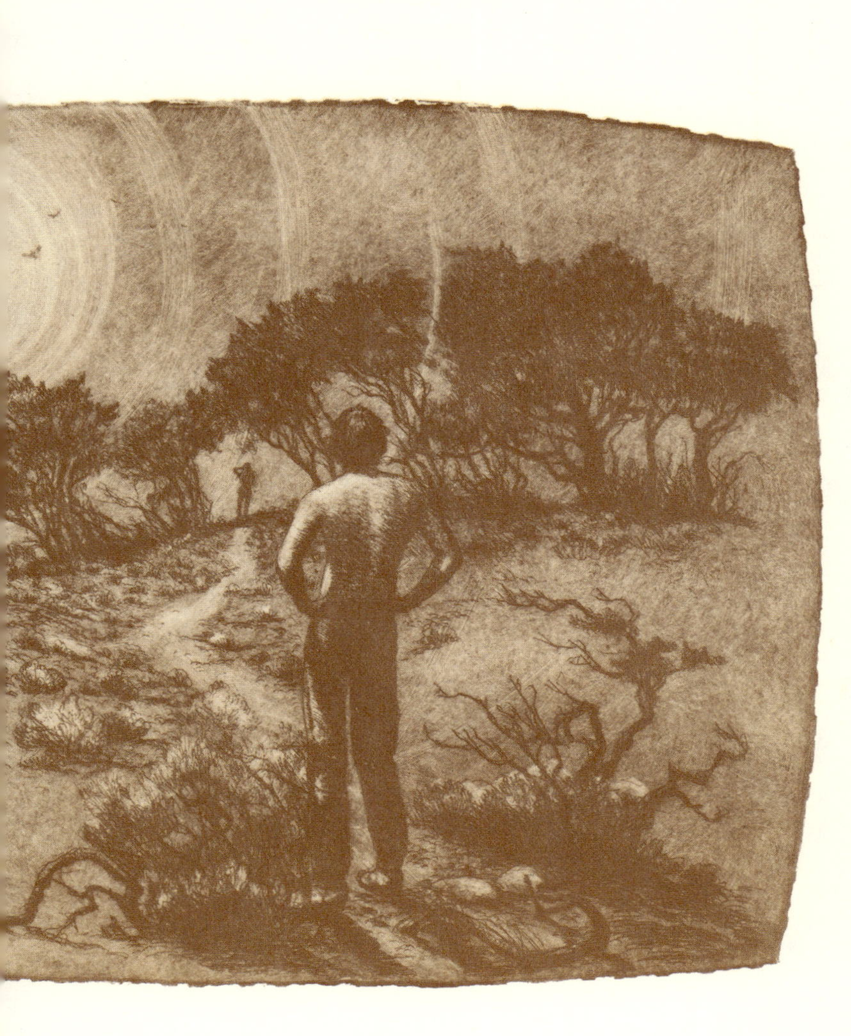

And down I plunged to search for answers
among the insane thoughts of voices
echoing my fears
voices inside my own
echoing in frightened ears
and the voices cried for language
a tongue with which to speak
a tool to pry my rusted doors
and open the mansions
built beyond my grasp
worlds within worlds
reflecting worlds without

And I wrote the fragile words
that burst themselves upon the shores
of consciousness
with frantic pen

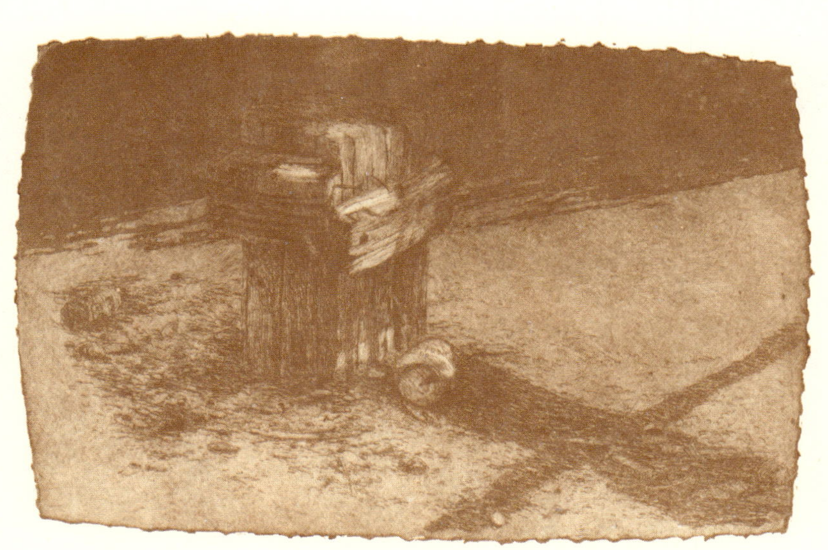

I uttered incoherent thoughts
until the voices crystalized
and framed themselves
in lines and forms
and fashioned tools to tear away
the barriers that bound my mind
and opened myself
to understand my dreams

The sun that warmed my soul
sang songs of sadness now to soothe my fears
and slowed the anger
that devoured my longing

I wandered alone over the soft earth
of my nothingness
a failure at response and education
learned and naive
educated within the walls of learning
but lacking wisdom
to answer questions
continuing to plague

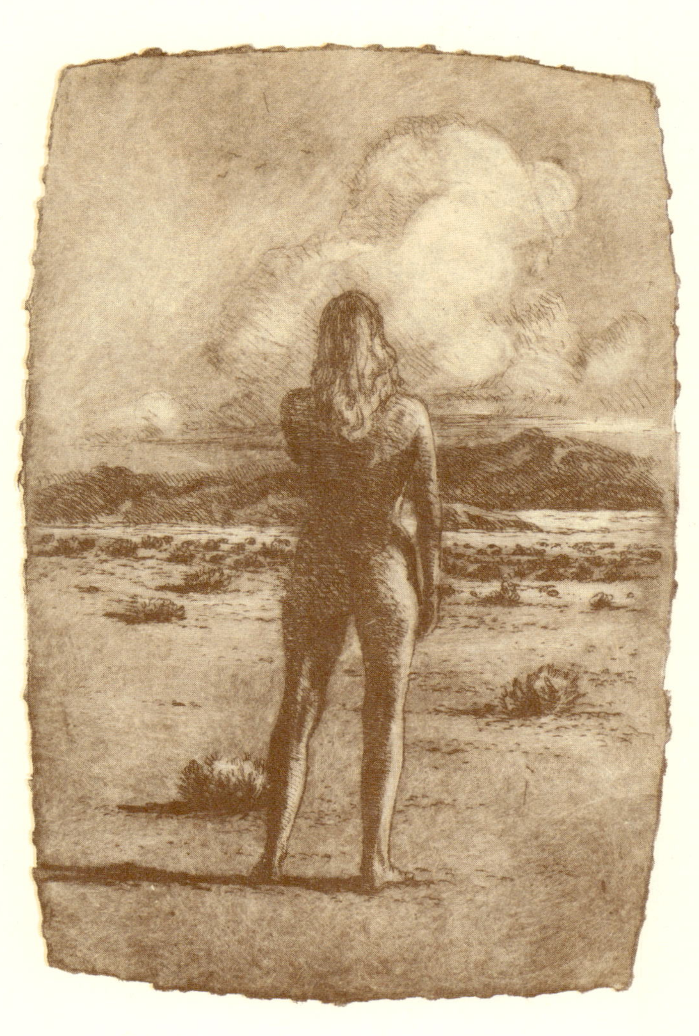

But the voices within
stirred the response of images
from depths beyond the scope
of books
and my mind searched the inner world
to discover the source of myth
cliffs of stone secured the images
writhing out of my darkness
to splash against the rocks
and the devouring serpent opened its mouth
to consume my sanity
giving birth to the forms
of the fears that held the torch
of my salvation

Chaos reigned
within the Pandora's box
of my personality
burst of its bonds
and frenzied prisoners bound
behind the walls of all my fears
leaped from darkness
into the golden light of day
overwhelming consciousness

Creation had emerged from the hand of God
a male ego on the waves of storm
born of the mind and the will of thought
and the world
had ordered darkness
into light

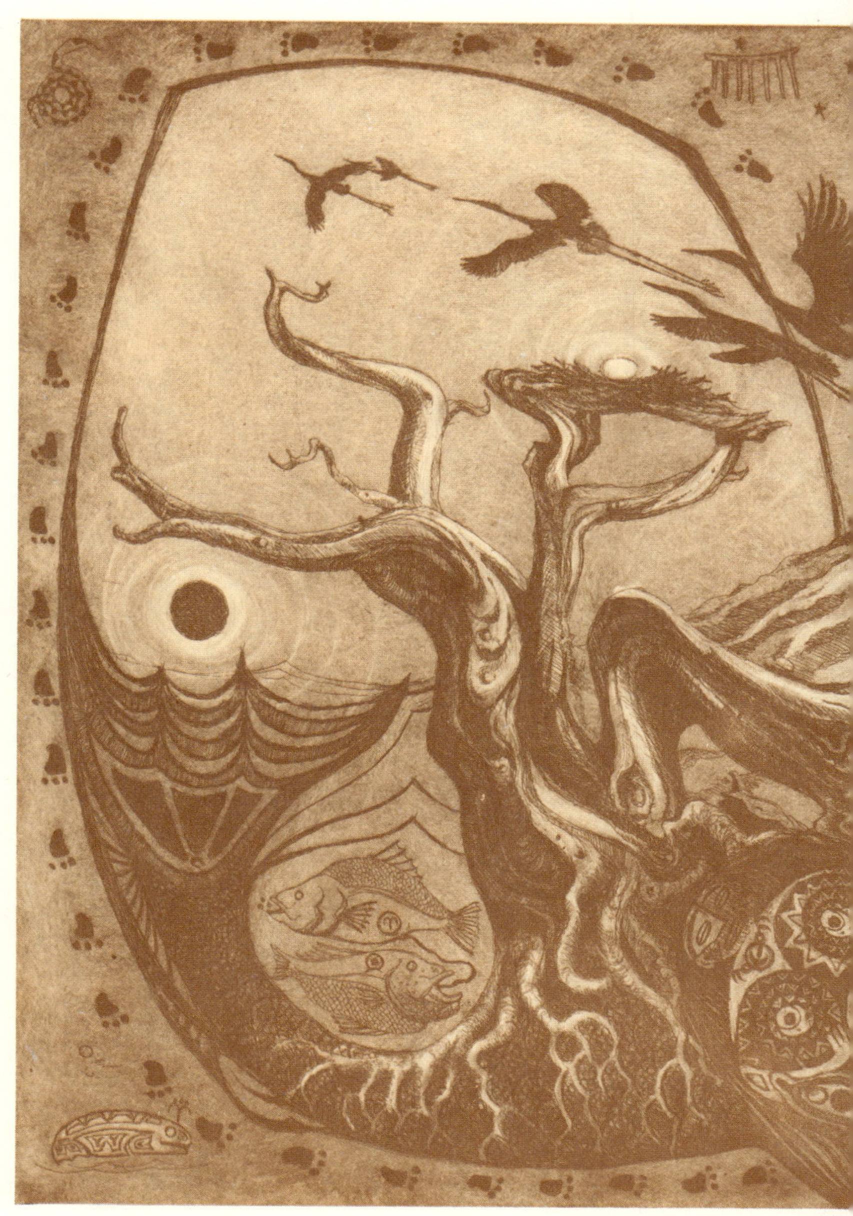

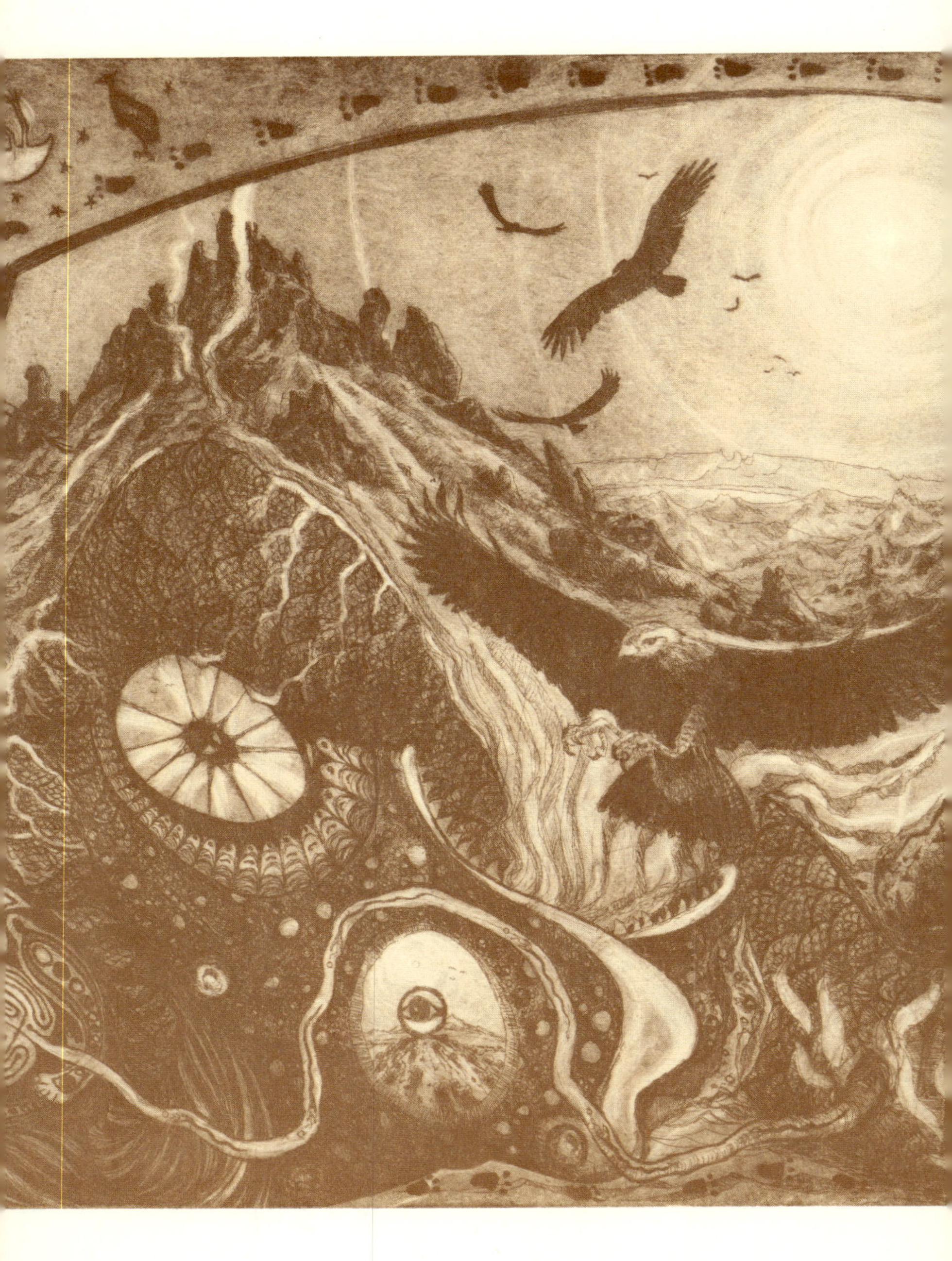

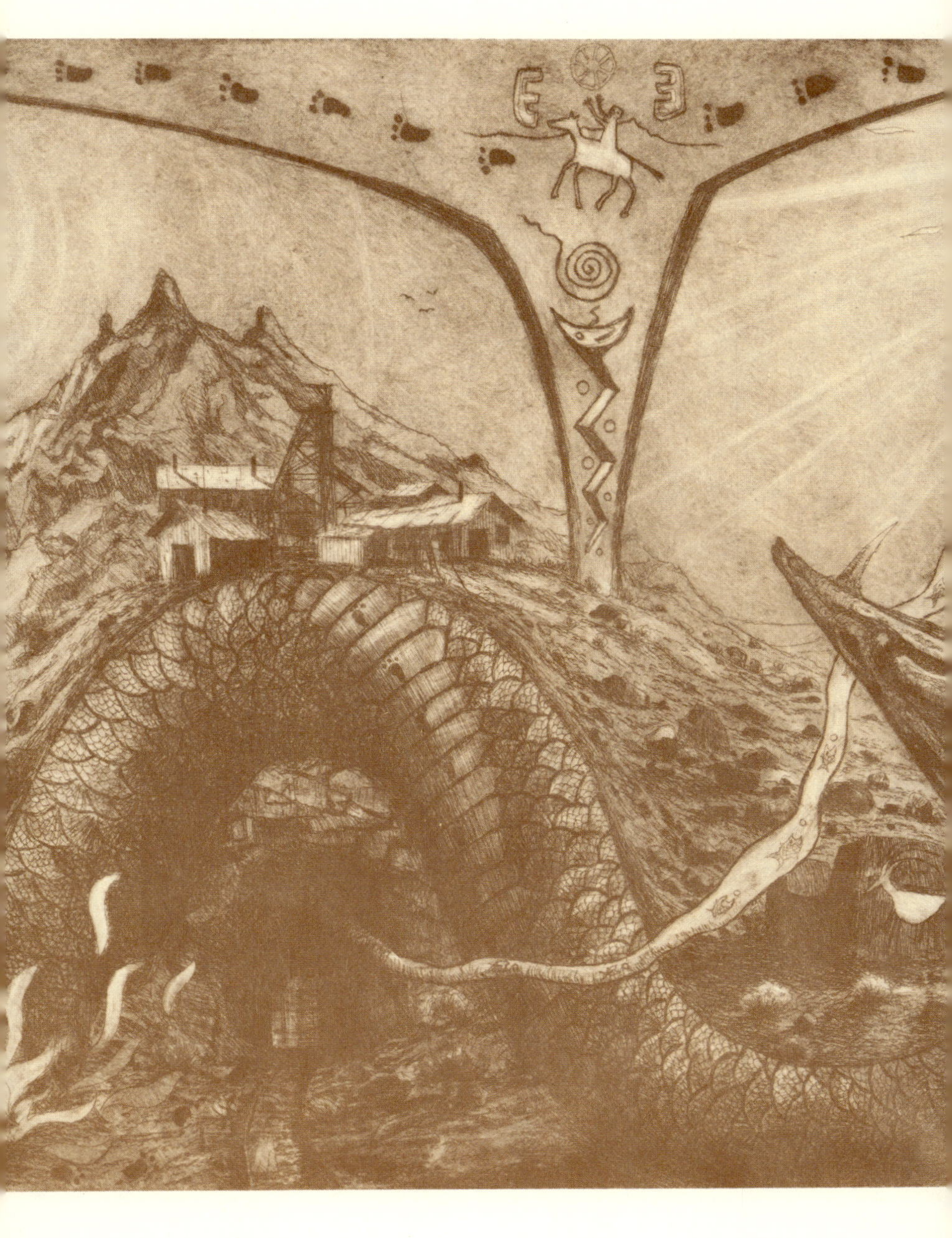

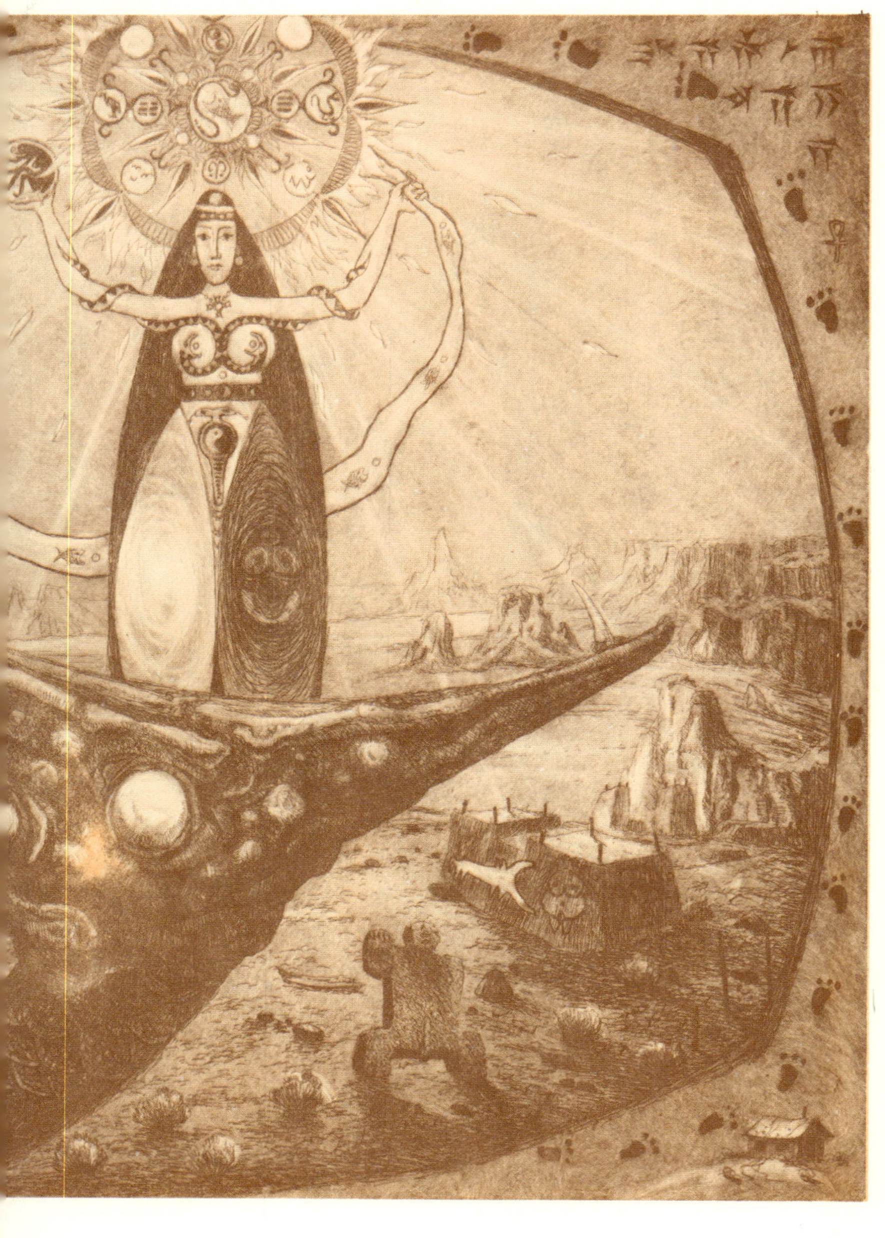

Crystal on the wings of intellect He stood
bellowing tradition from the holy mount
and carving His worship
on the cliffs of my coming
from every holy text and training
down the halls of church
my mind was fed to pray
out of darkness to the giver
of the light of day

And now
I stood too proud to bow
on bended knee
to the cold idea of a god
I'd never see
and from the battleground of fear's security
I fled
following dreams that held my course
to take a darker road
and run beyond the boundaries
of my faith

I burned the cross that cradled me
fashioned my own of crooked sticks
and bone
and thanking Jesus
took my burden from His heavy hands
and walked
into the storm

The Mother
dark and brooding
unconscious womb of life
had been expelled from heaven

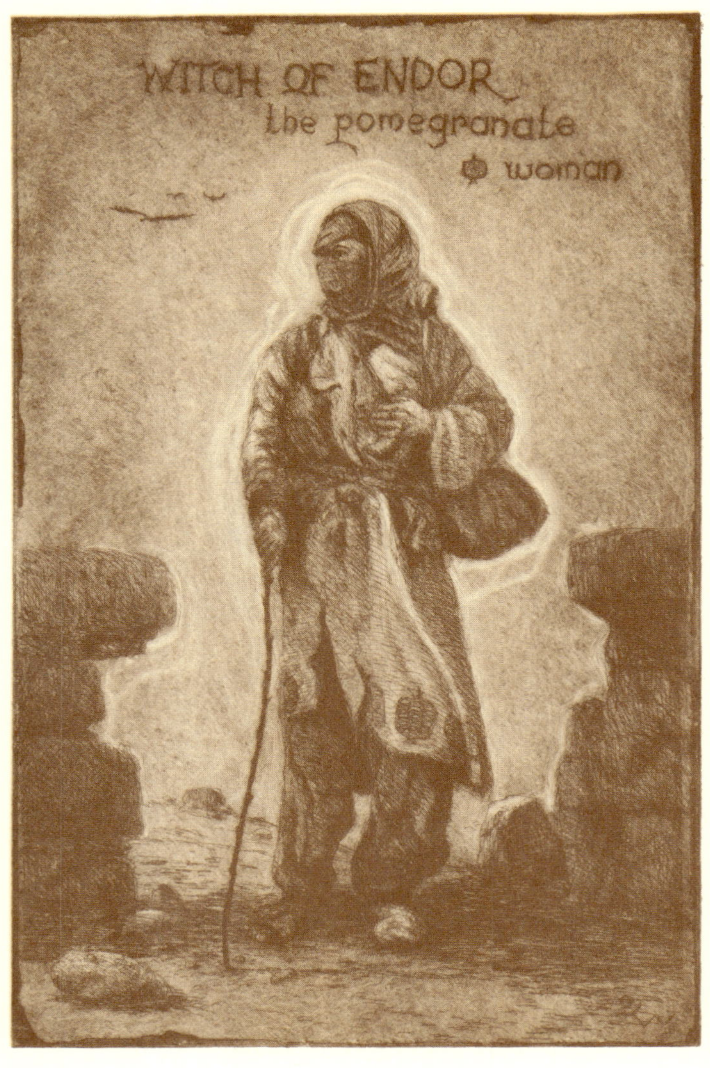

cursed to trudge in her travail
down the centuries of man
to be revealed
only through the moons of dream
and when I ran into that holy darkness
filled with fright
dodging the fears of lightning
flung from an angry god
jealous of his gifts usurped by night
I found her opening wide her womb
revealing eggs fertility
and the birth of pure creativity
goddess of the golden tree
keeper of cycles from the depths
of sea
and the rebirth of forms
fulfilling themselves
in a pregnant seed
and the need to restore her throne
robbed me of rest
blessed me with the curse
of revelation
as the need for the reconciliation
of my troubled soul
echoed the psychic split
of a gone world
and the holy darkness lured me on
to reveal her fullness
bringing the land of dreams
into the dawn

Volumes of Jung relieved my ignorance
and I plunged my phallic mind
into the fertile depths
of a rich subconscious sea

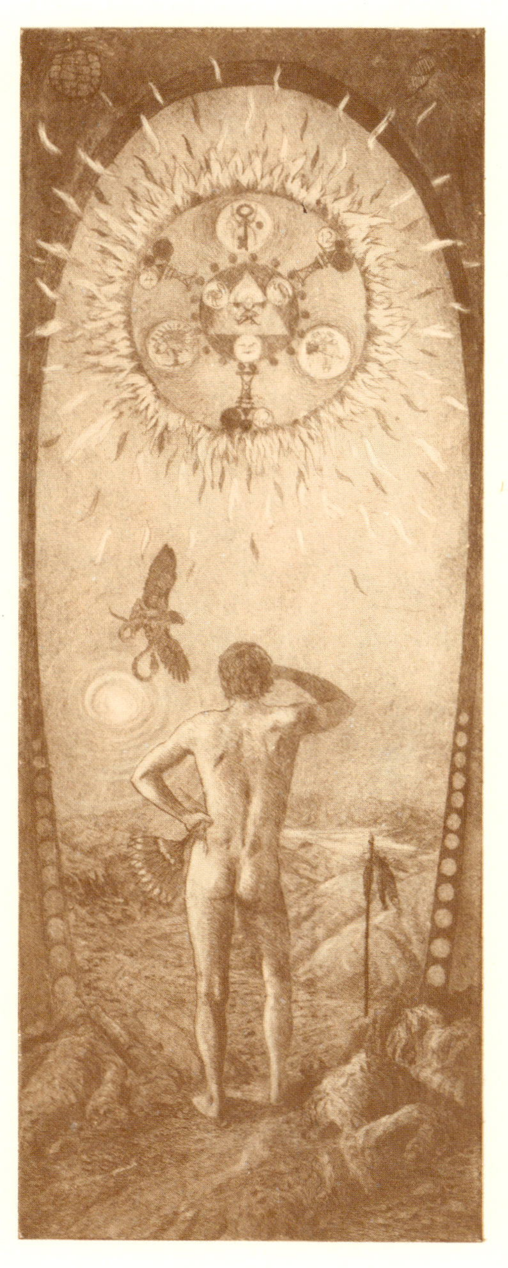

deeper and deeper until tears answered tears
beyond the years of feeling
and I knew that fear would never
hold me close again
the chains dissolved
the walls succumbed
and I faced the black Minotaur
of love
within the maze of my being
the devouring feminine
released
built by the fears within the fears
that chased me down the years of youth
and there
erected Her upon the pedestal
of puberty
unapproachable
untouchable
except in violence

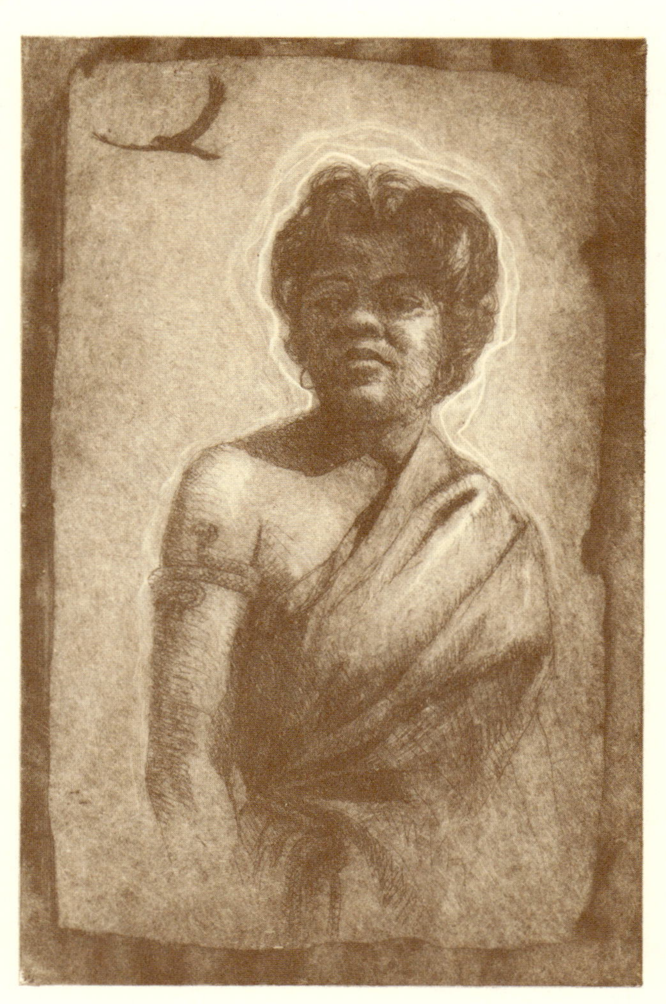

Afraid
and fragile as a butterfly
that suns its newborn wings
to glide upon the wind
I fluttered into the love
that hungered for expression
hovered upon the hurricane
and let the bond
become a bondage
breeding the tendrils of passion
that would wind themselves
into the cracks and crannies
of the carefully constructed walls
that bound me in my fears

And when they reached
the base of my being
wound around my heart
I turned and ran
ripping out my years of heaviness
and screamed my agony to the moon
that hung in silver
tattered threads
from a shredded soul

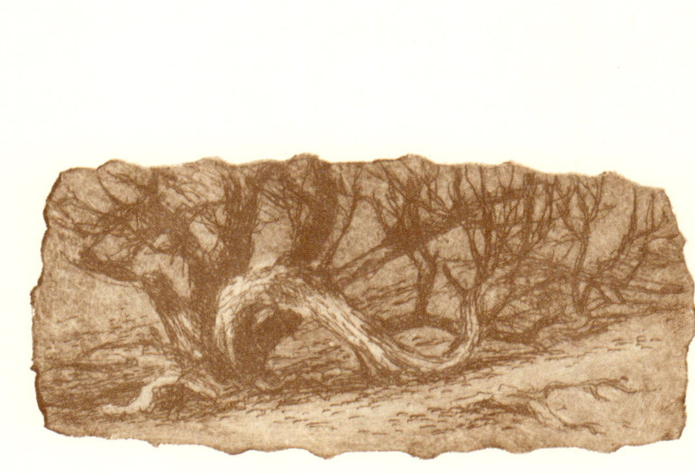

I sang my loneliness and pain
down the dark deserted halls
of the hells through which
I walked
trying to liberate illusion
from reality
and return the woman
to her role of love
hoping to live
without the reconstruction
of the walls
born of pain
that lay in rubble
at my bleeding feet
washed by my reign
of tears

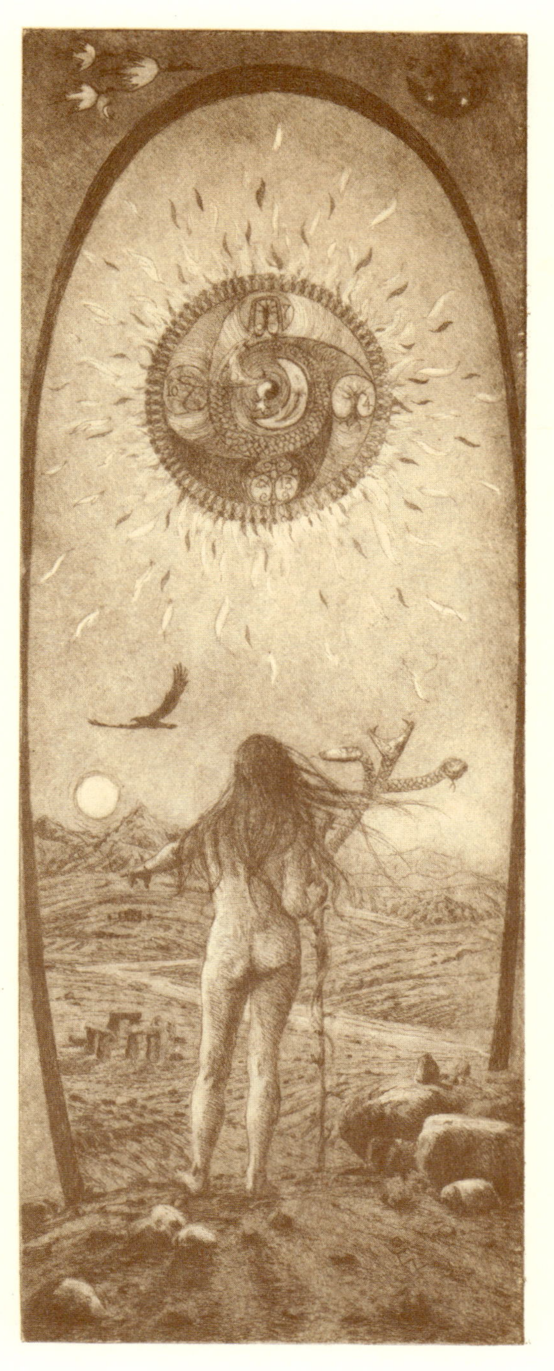

I would have drawn a sword
rushed to her dark throne
and plunged it
into her enveloping softness
but she emerged in silence
from the smouldering rubble
threw off the scales that burdened my vision
and stood before me in eternal beauty
Anima Mundi
mistress of the holy mountain
guardian of the whirlwind
and reached out to take
my hand

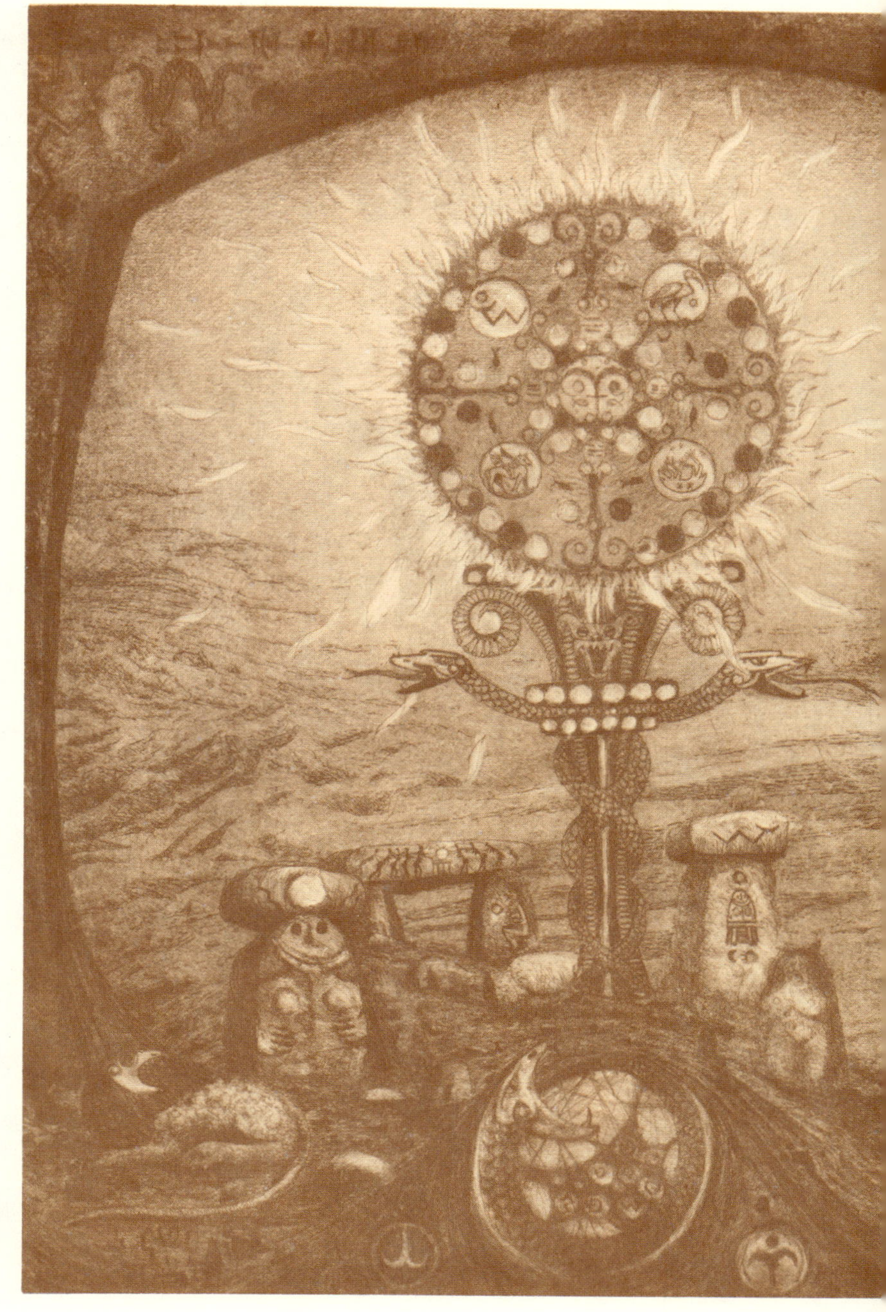

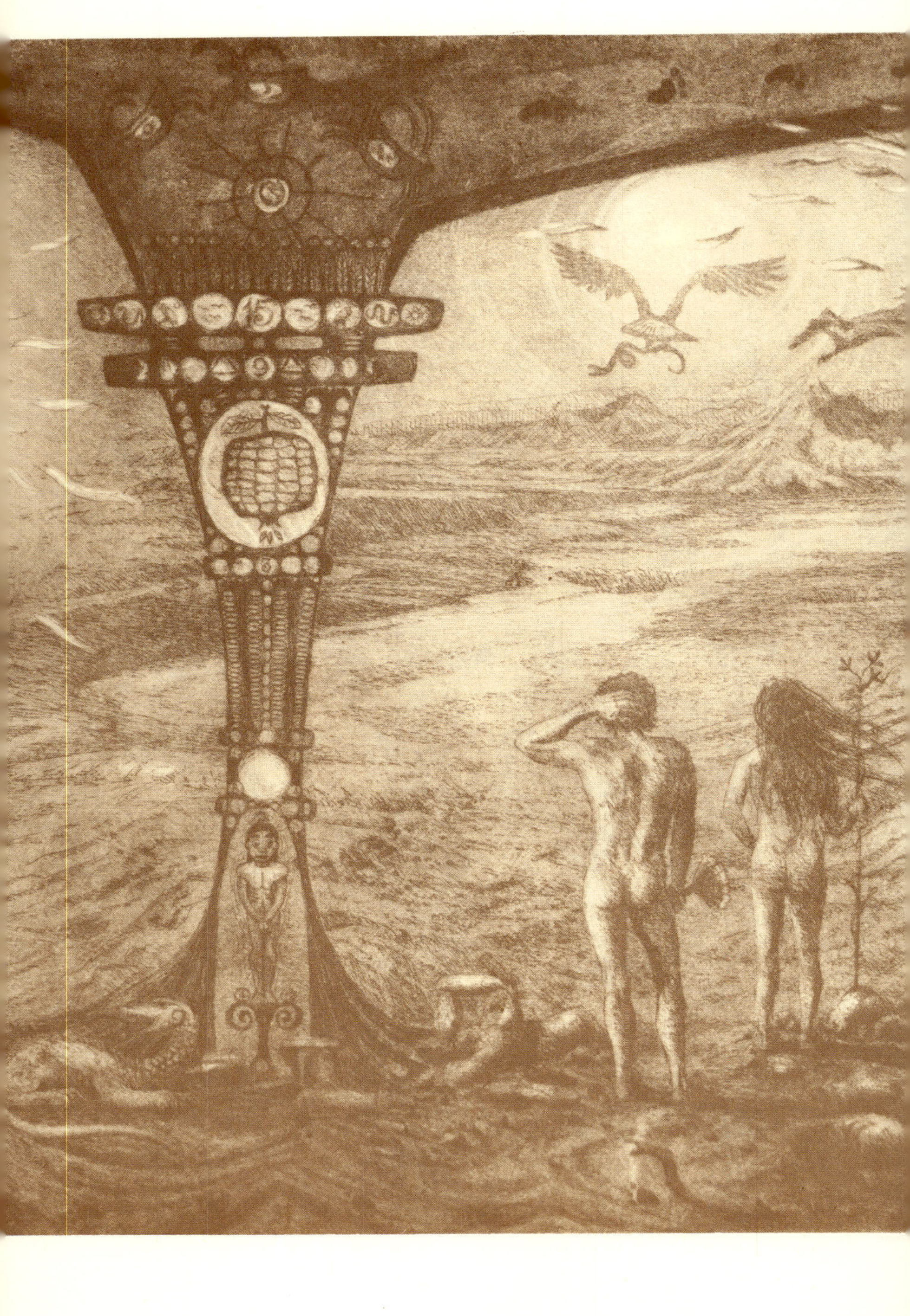

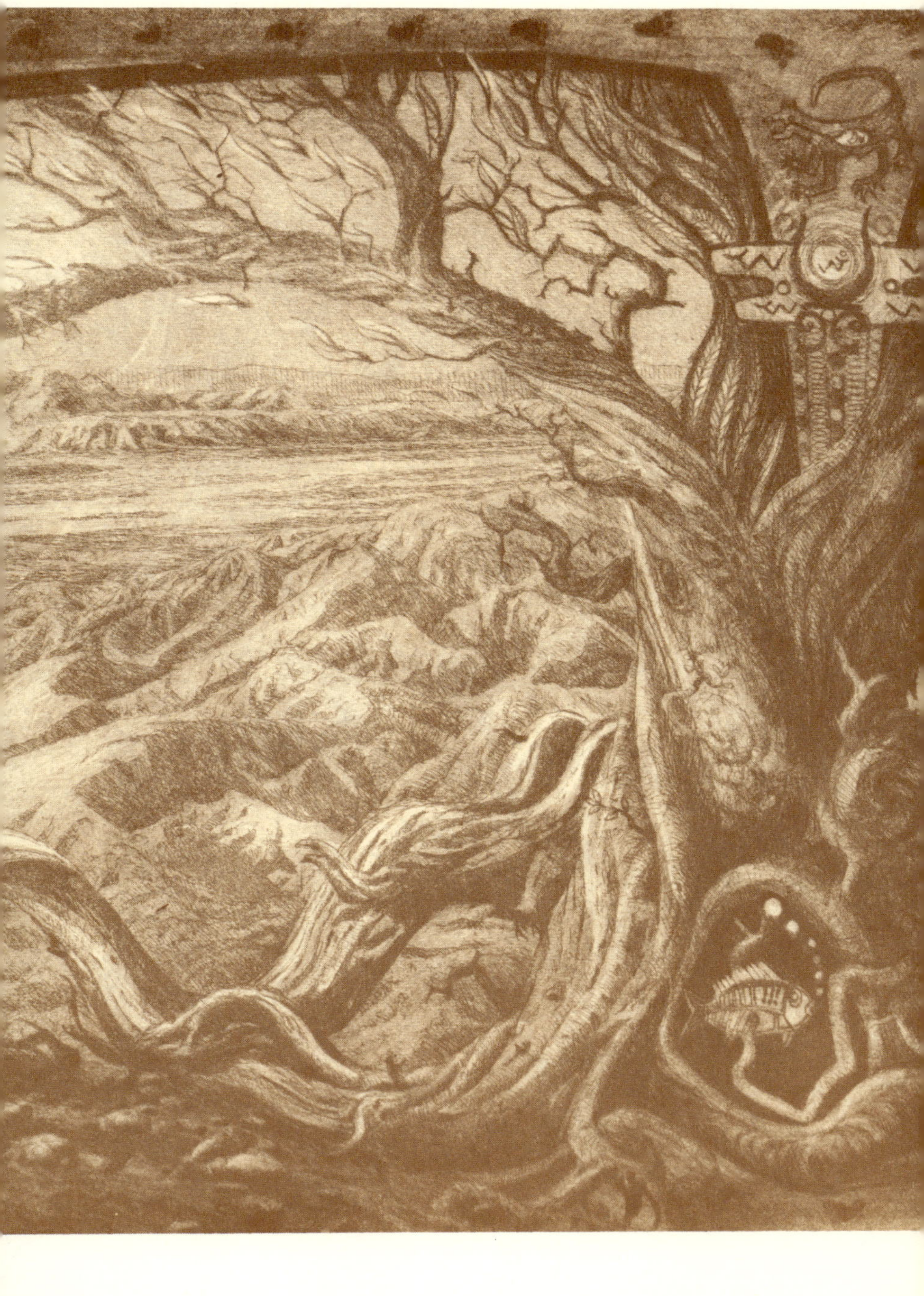

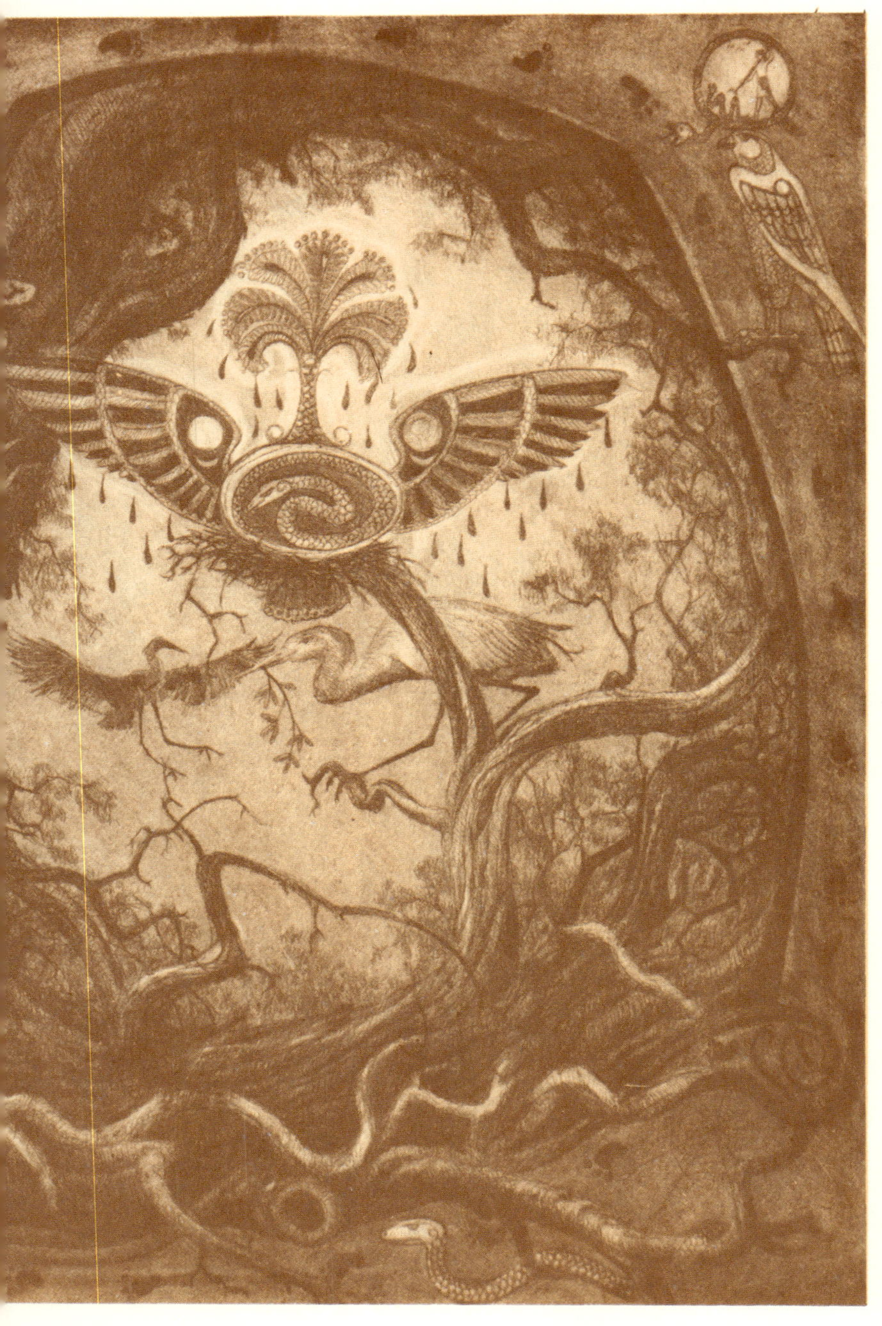

Now amid the buds of spring
in the green valley we walk
myself and I
Adam and Eve
learning to know each other
through the memory
of our having found ourselves
in that eternal moment
of our coming

male and female
in a holy marriage
born of fear and passion
and the need to know
we speak to each other
with the speech of love
and moisten each other's lips
with tears that wash away
the fears of yesterday
and stand in silence
in the holy land of dreams
feeling beyond the fear to feel
and full of tenderness
within the structured walls of time
and being
what we are
to make our Journey

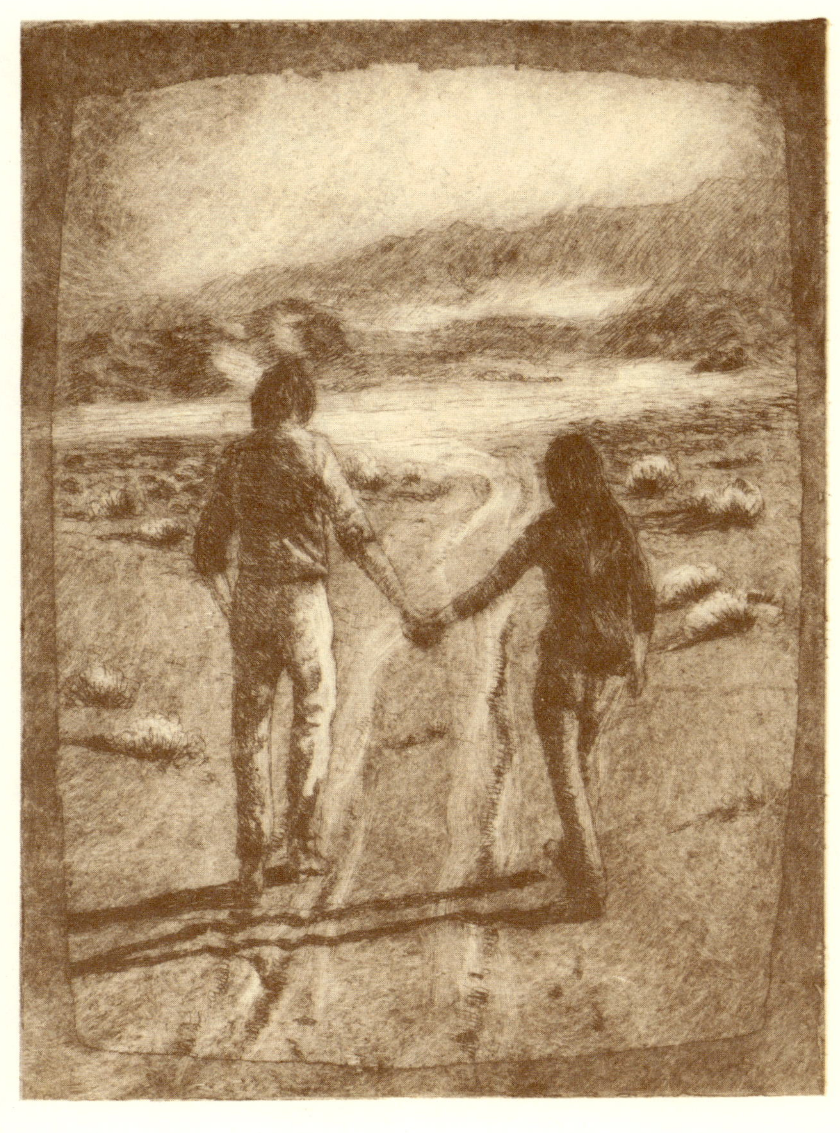

Dedicated to Little Roy
whose Journey in this life
has ended

Today
his little body sleeps
returned to the earth
that gave it birth
his spirit departed

I will hear him laughing
in the wind
that comes to explore the canyons
of my lonely soul
will see him running
down the sandwash deserts
of my dying
will find myself crying
when I embrace him
in the warm arms
of my imagination
and mirror the memory
of his laughing face
in the still waters
of my longing.

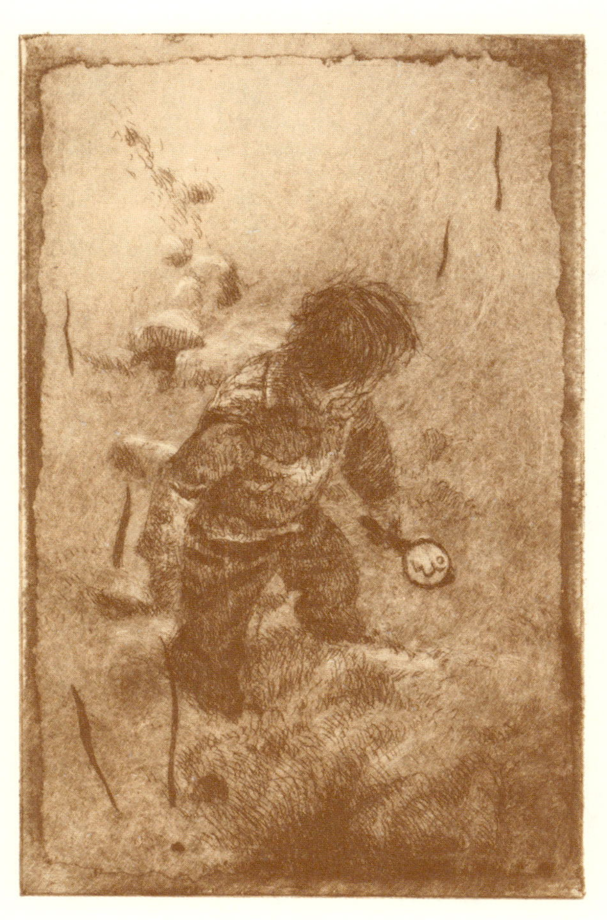

OTHER BOOKS OF INTEREST FROM CELESTIAL ARTS

THE ESSENCE OF ALAN WATTS. The basic philosophy of Alan Watts in nine illustrated volumes. Now available:

GOD. 64 pages, paper, $3.95

MEDITATION. 64 pages, paper, $3.95

NOTHINGNESS. 64 pages, paper, $3.95

TIME. 64 pages, paper, $3.95

DEATH. 64 pages, paper, $3.95

THE NATURE OF MAN. 64 pages, paper, $3.95

WILL I THINK OF YOU. Leonard Nimoy's warm and compelling sequel to You & I. 96 pages, paper, $3.95

THE HUMANNESS OF YOU, Vol. I & Vol. II. Walt Rinder's philosophy rendered in his own words and photographs. Each: 64 pages, paper, $2.95.

MY DEAREST FRIEND. The compassion and sensitivity that marked Walt Rinder's previous works are displayed again in this beautiful new volume. 64 pages, paper, $2.95.

ONLY ONE TODAY. Walt Rinder's widely acclaimed style is again apparent in this beautifully illustrated poem. 64 pages, paper, $2.95

THE HEALING MIND by Dr. Irving Oyle. A noted physician describes what is known about the mysterious ability of the mind to heal the body. 128 pages, cloth, $7.95; paper, $4.95.

I WANT TO BE USED not abused by Ed Branch. How to adapt to the demands of others and gain more pleasure from relationships. 80 pages, paper, $2.95.

INWARD JOURNEY Art and Psychotherapy For You by Margaret Keyes. A therapist demonstrates how anyone can use art as a healing device. 128 pages, paper, $4.95.

PLEASE TRUST ME by James Vaughan. A simple, illustrated book of poetry about the quality too often lacking in our experiences—Trust. 64 pages, paper, $2.95.

LOVE IS AN ATTITUDE. The world-famous book of poetry and photographs by Walter Rinder. 128 pages, cloth, $7.95; paper, $3.95.

THIS TIME CALLED LIFE. Poetry and photography by Walter Rinder. 160 pages, cloth, $7.95; paper, $3.95.

SPECTRUM OF LOVE. Walter Rinder's remarkable love poem with magnificently enhancing drawings by David Mitchell. 64 pages, cloth, $7.95; paper, $2.95.

GROWING TOGETHER. George and Donni Betts' poetry with photographs by Robert Scales. 128 pages, paper, $3.95.

VISIONS OF YOU. Poems by George Betts, with photographs by Robert Scales. 128 pages, paper, $3.95.

MY GIFT TO YOU. New poems by George Betts, with photographs by Robert Scales. 128 pages, paper, $3.95.

YOU & I. Leonard Nimoy, the distinguished actor, blends his poetry and photography into a beautiful love story. 128 pages, cloth, $7.95; paper, $3.95.

I AM. Concepts of awareness in poetic form by Michael Grinder. Illustrated in color by Chantal. 64 pages, paper, $2.95.

GAMES STUDENTS PLAY (And what to do about them.) A study of Transactional Analysis in schools, by Kenneth Ernst. 128 pages, cloth, $7.95; paper, $3.95.

A GUIDE FOR SINGLE PARENTS (Transactional Analysis for People in Crisis.) T.A. for single parents by Kathryn Hallett. 128 pages, cloth, $7.95; paper, $3.95.

THE PASSIONATE MIND (A Manual for Living Creatively with One's Self.) Guidance and understanding from Joel Kramer. 128 pages, paper, $3.95.

COVER and BOOK DESIGN by MAREK A. MAJEWSKI